T0121928

THE KEY TO

Unl**o**cking

THE CLOSET DOOR

A Coming-Out Guide on a Journey toward Unconditional Self-Love

Chelsea Griffo, LMSW

BALBOA.
PRESS
A DIVISION OF HAY HOUSE

Balboa Press books may be ordered through booksellers or by contacting:

Balboa Press
A Division of Hay House
1663 Liberty Drive
Bloomington, IN 47403
www.balboapress.com
1 (877) 407-4847

Because of the dynamic nature of the Internet, any web addresses or links contained in this book may have changed since publication and may no longer be valid. The views expressed in this work are solely those of the author and do not necessarily reflect the views of the publisher, and the publisher hereby disclaims any responsibility for them.

The author of this book does not dispense medical advice or prescribe the use of any technique as a form of treatment for physical, emotional, or medical problems without the advice of a physician, either directly or indirectly. The intent of the author is only to offer information of a general nature to help you in your quest for emotional and spiritual well-being. In the event you use any of the information in this book for yourself, which is your constitutional right, the author and the publisher assume no responsibility for your actions.

Any people depicted in stock imagery provided by Thinkstock are models, and such images are being used for illustrative purposes only.
Certain stock imagery © Thinkstock.

Printed in the United States of America.

ISBN: 978-1-4525-9213-8 (sc)
ISBN: 978-1-4525-9214-5 (hc)
ISBN: 978-1-4525-9212-1 (e)

Library of Congress Control Number: 2014902378

Balboa Press rev. date: 9/5/2014

This book is dedicated to my mother,
who continues to teach me what it
truly means to love unconditionally.

And a day came when the risk it took
to stay tight in a bud was more painful
than the risk it took to blossom.
—Anais Nin

and perhaps arrange a few blind dates with some of her very sophisticated friends.

Though I never found the book back then, Chelsea Griffo is my new favorite "real live gay lady," and you are reading the book I wish I'd found. (And the dating advice is in chapter 18!) Yay!

You are loved,
Karen McCrocklin

Preface

I feel deeply grateful and honored to have the privilege of writing this powerful and unique coming-out guide. When I was beginning my coming-out journey, I knew of very few gay people, and I did not have anyone in my life who even remotely understood what I was going through. There were no books to be found that discussed how to navigate the internal process that many gay people first experience, moving from shame, guilt, and fear to joy, pride, contentment, and eventually unconditional self-love. This guide is intended to be a beacon of hope to those who are in the process of coming out and are in need of advice and direction on which steps to take next. My main objective is to provide answers to some of the universal questions we all have when first coming out, as well as to offer tools and strategies for developing a healthy self-image and unconditional self-love.

I came out during the process of obtaining my master's degree in clinical social work and, with the goal of meeting more gay people, I took it upon myself to form a student group called Prism for LGBTQ Catholics and allies. This provided me with many opportunities to coach Catholic friends of mine through their own coming-out processes and to help them learn that they are perfect exactly as they are, no matter what they may have been taught by society or religion. I also had the opportunity to volunteer as a support-group facilitator for LGBTQ teens at an organization called OutYouth in Austin, Texas.

After college, I continued to have old friends approach me with questions about coming out, looking for support from someone who understood their experience. As a result of this, I made the decision to create the book I had been searching for so many years ago, so that I could share the wisdom I have gained from my own coming-out journey with anyone courageous enough to take the next steps on their own path toward honoring and loving who they truly are.

Throughout this writing, I have intentionally used gender-neutral language, such as "they" and "them" as often as possible, out of respect for the great variance in gender identity and expression to be found in our vibrant community. It should also be noted that the terms *gay, LGBT, LGBTQ,* and *queer* are all used interchangeably to refer to and include the entire LGBTQ community whenever mentioned, because saying "lesbian, gay, bisexual, transgender, queer, intersex, androgynous, asexual, and questioning" can become a mouthful after a while.

I want to help people realize that being gay, lesbian, bisexual, transgender (and everything else in between) is a fantastic gift. My primary inspiration has come from my own life experiences leading up to this point and is necessarily personal at times. When writing about something as intimate as coming out, it is crucial to be as authentic as possible. Though everyone's coming-out process is different, there are many universal experiences that we share as lesbian, gay, bisexual, transgender, and queer people, and it is my hope that I can provide a point of reference for this experience from which most people will be able to draw comfort and hope on their own journey.

Introduction

The Reason for This Guide

Fear. It's that ever-present ache or tingling in your stomach; the blood rushing to your face and the adrenaline burst that floods your body every time someone asks you a seemingly normal, non-threatening question you know you cannot answer honestly. Fear is the voice in your head that tells you, "They say they're my friends, but that's because they don't know. My family says they love me no matter what, but ... what if my secret is the exception?" Fear causes us to keep our mouths shut when a homophobic joke, comment, or slur is said right to our faces, pushing our anger and hurt down where no one can see, while we die a little inside. Fear can sometimes even turn us into one of those people, bullying others verbally or physically in order to avoid letting others discover who we truly are.

This is the fear I felt the night I finally admitted to myself that I was gay. Sitting alone in my college apartment, I struggled to say the words "I'm a lesbian" out loud. I'm not sure whether it was the crippling anxiety or continuous sobbing that prevented me, but no matter how I tried, I couldn't force those words out of my mouth. I had been denying and suppressing my true sexual identity since fifth grade, and the floodgates had finally burst wide open.

Although I had many friends and supportive family members in my life at the time, this was the one problem I knew I couldn't ask them to help me with. I needed them more than I ever had, and they were the very people to whom I was most afraid to reveal my sexuality. The fear of losing them was just too great. So I went in search of a book to help me learn how to come out. *How do you find other gay people? How do I come out to my family? Are all of the emotions I'm feeling normal? Are there any other gay people like me?*

I found several books about LGBT history, famous gay people, and how to have gay sex. I also learned where the rainbow flag and the upside-down-triangle symbol came from, but none of these books addressed the fears I had or gave me any practical action steps for coming out. They certainly didn't talk about all of the great things about being gay or how to overcome the negative ideas and beliefs that society had ingrained in my head about what it means to be gay. Most of what I have learned about coming out came from trial and error, but I had a wonderful therapy group to support me through it. The fuel that kept me going was the simple, insatiable desire to one day feel comfortable in my own skin and not only to be able to be myself without fear or shame, but to *love* being exactly who I was born to be.

Living in fear is dark, lonely, and soul-crushing, and can make it very hard to see any light in the future, but there comes a time when this prison of fear becomes too hard to stand any longer. We all came into this world as perfect, whole, and beautiful beings, whose only purpose in life is to love ourselves and others and spend our time doing what excites our souls and brings joy to our hearts. This book is a guide to remembering how to do that, and its intention is to be like spiritual fertilizer for your soul, to help it blossom and burst out of its dark prison of fear into the sunlight. It is about love and forgiveness—for others, but most importantly for ourselves. Coming out is about setting our souls free with self-love and learning to become independent of the opinions of other people.

Being gay is one of the best things that could have happened to me, because it has allowed me to grow as a human being in ways that few other experiences ever could. One day, you may be so fortunate as to have the opportunity to support friends who began their coming-out journeys after you did, and having lived it, you will be able to help coach them through it. There are few things as inspiring as watching people grow in love for themselves and stop basing their self-worth on what other people think of them. This guide is entitled "A Journey toward Unconditional Self-Love" because that is exactly what the act of coming out is all about. By making the decision to come out, you are telling yourself and everyone else that you are perfect just the way you are, and it is such a great thing that you just have to share it with the rest of the world. (Or maybe just the important people. It's up to you!)

I hope this book can help lift you up, give you hope, empower you to keep going through the hard times, and get to the pot of gold at the end of the rainbow. (Pun intended.) Once you get through the most challenging parts of coming out to yourself, to family, and to close friends, it just gets easier and easier. Some people reading this right now might think that no one in the world could really love you for exactly who you are, but you *are* loved, whether you want to believe it or not. I love you with all of my heart, and that is the reason I have written this book.

Chapter 1

Coming Out to Myself

If I had to pick an age, I guess you could say that I officially came out to myself at the age of twenty-one. I kissed a girl for the first time in a pub in Rome, Italy, on a college study-abroad trip, while my best friend was in the bathroom … and it was awesome. This would not be quite true, though, because the first time I kissed a girl happened long before that. It would be more accurate to say that this was my first girl kiss without any negative social consequences. After my first couple of innocent attempts to kiss girls, it took a decade for me to overcome the shame that was ingrained in my psyche by the outside world and to find the courage to give my natural instincts a chance again.

I grew up in a small Texas town in a Catholic family. There were no gay people in my life at all, and I never learned anything about them from anyone in my family. As a little kid, I was a pretty stereotypical tomboy. I loved climbing trees, playing soccer with the boys at recess, and I could not stand Barbie dolls. Despite the fact that I wanted to learn the piano more than anything, play soccer, or learn to tap dance, my dad put me on a softball team in second grade, for which I became very grateful later in life. It never really occurred to me that I was different from any other kid, and my parents generally encouraged me to express myself the way I wanted.

In a perfect world, without judgment or homophobia, I'm sure that my sexuality would have developed naturally, without me having to "discover" anything about myself. The first memory I have of becoming aware of my same-sex attraction was in fifth grade. I was ten years old, and I was playing basketball with my friend Allison in the gym at school. She was a very special friend to me, and that day, I suddenly felt the impulse to kiss her on the cheek. It wasn't anything I had planned out; it just seemed like the most natural thing in the world in that moment. To my surprise, Allison got angry at me and wiped her hand across her cheek. I stood there, confused and a little hurt. I could not understand why a kiss would make her so mad … but I never kissed her again.

The next school year, I had new friends and had pretty much forgotten about kissing Allison. As an eleven-year-old, I still wasn't too conscious of the changes beginning to happen in my body. It certainly never occurred to me to slap a label on the new emotions I was feeling or that I had anything to hide. One day, I was in the hallway with my friend Julie, when that same impulsive urge came over me. Again, without any premeditated thought, but simply acting on the innocent emotions I felt toward her, I kissed Julie on the cheek. Julie's reaction was different than Allison's, though. Allison had been angry, but Julie just stared at me with a look of disgust on her face.

As the next few days, weeks, and months began to unfold, I started to notice people staring at me in the hallways at school. Sometimes I would catch them whispering to each other and looking at me, quickly turning away when we made eye contact. Julie told people that I was a lesbian. I didn't know what that meant, but I knew it must have been bad because of the way everyone was treating me. That was when it began to sink in that Allison and Julie were not the only ones who thought it was bad for a girl to kiss another girl. Apparently, everyone thought that. One of the lessons that stuck with me the most during my junior high and high school education was that wanting to kiss or hold hands with a girl was not only wrong but worthy of making you a complete social outcast. I even had a math teacher who made a comment about two girls he had seen holding hands in the hallway. "It's disgusting," he said.

All of the extremely negative feedback and bullying I received from kissing Julie was easily enough to send me deep into the closet for the next decade. I continued to be taught time and again by teachers, friends, church people, and family members that being gay was not okay. It was almost impossible to count how many times you would hear gay slurs in just one day of school. Kids were constantly using *gay* as a substitute word for any negative adjective or calling someone a fag just because they stepped outside of their gender norm for a second.

Denial combined with fear is a very powerful thing, and I put my heart and soul into convincing myself that I was not gay. Once in sixth grade, I even slapped myself on the school bus when the thought of kissing another girl popped into my head and turned me on. I became extremely active in school clubs and band, and I was always buried in homework. I was too busy to even think about dating anyone, and that was exactly how I wanted it. Also, it's pretty easy to avoid thinking about dating anyway, when your only option is to date someone of the opposite sex and you are not the least bit interested. Now and then, I was able to convince myself that I had a crush on a boy, who was usually just a close friend that I felt safe around. Either that or he was already taken, and I would not have to worry about him wanting to date me.

I always thought that I did a pretty good job of hiding the fact that I was gay, but some of the fashion trends I went through from sixth to twelfth grade may have been a clue to some of my friends and more open-minded family members. From fifth grade through seventh, I wore a vest to school literally every single day. (Vests were "in" back in the '90s, okay!) When I was about to enter seventh grade, a new rule said that we had to tuck in our shirts, and I was so worried that they would make me tuck in my vests. I didn't want to look like a nerd! To my extreme relief, my mom went with me to talk to my school guidance counselor, who assured me that I would not have to tuck in my vests. How my sweet mother was able to keep a straight face (no pun intended) during that conversation with the counselor, I will never know.

My mom was always good about letting me pick out my own clothes, in order to build my self-esteem, but she did try to influence my fashion decisions from time to time. Once she took me to a super-trendy store, back when bell bottoms were just coming back into style. She told me I could pick out anything I wanted in the entire store, and she would buy it for me. The pressure was on, but I couldn't find a single thing I liked. Finally, I grabbed a lime-green Mickey Mouse T-shirt off a rack. It was obviously too big, but it was the only thing in the whole store that I was even remotely interested in. Reluctant and a little disappointed, my mom brought the shirt to the checkout counter.

Following the vest phase was the polo shirt and khaki shorts phase, my baseball jersey phase, and the overalls phase. One time, my friends Erich and Greg actually took me to Starbucks and flat out asked me if I was a lesbian, to which I defensively replied, "No! Of course not! Why would you think that?" They never answered my question.

Although I stayed in denial for about ten years, every five years or so, I would have an intense identity crisis well up inside me. *Oh God, I think I might be gay! No, I can't be gay. I'm not "like that!"* The thought of what that could mean for my life was just too scary to handle at the time. Fear has an amazing way of convincing your mind to deny what you know to be true in your heart, and it amazes me how creative I would get to believe I was straight for a little while longer. The problem was, each time I had one of these identity crises, it became more and more difficult to manipulate my mind back into a state of relieved denial. As a nineteen-year-old college freshman, I had another one of those anxiety-filled heart-to-heart talks with my soul, and I actually wrote a prayer in my journal, asking God to help me not be gay. By the end of the entry, I had somehow come to the conclusion again that I was straight, but that was the last time I was ever able to do it. Here is my journal entry from that day:

2/17/2004
Dear God,

I know that you've always known that this has bothered me since the fifth grade, but I need to talk about it anyway. I'm not quite sure why, but I've been so afraid that I could be a lesbian. It's just that I've never really liked boys the way everyone else likes them. I never thought of all the movie star guys as being "hot" or felt all "wooo" about any of it. I felt like I'd really have a crush on a guy, but if he ever tried to get closer to me, the feeling would go away whenever he was around. I've been thinking about it so much, and I've realized that it's very hard for me to trust guys, men, whatever, and I have always just felt safe and comfortable and loved when I'm with girls. I don't really think that would make me a lesbian, but I feel like I just want my girlfriends to hold me in their arms because I know they care about me. I've never really met a guy who I could trust with my emotions in that way, who loves me so completely and totally and would never want anyone but me. Is there a man like this for me? I would be the happiest person on the face of the Earth if this dream could come true for me. Well, I guess I really do want a guy, huh? I'm just scared, but I don't need to be scared if you are the one to bring us together. I know you have a plan for me and that I just need to trust in you. I know you'll never let me down. I just wish I knew what the plan was, but I guess if you give away all the surprises, it wouldn't be as fun and wonderful when they unexpectedly happen. Thanks for making me feel better.

Love,
Chelsea

It's interesting how the ignorant opinions of other people can subconsciously become your own. However, it was the last good excuse I could think of to convince myself that I was just afraid to be in a relationship with a guy: "I just hadn't found the right one yet." Interestingly enough, it was shortly after this time that I met my first boyfriend, and our relationship lasted for about eight months. It was a very confusing experience for me. He was not a repulsive person at all, but the thought of kissing him always made me feel a little nauseated. I remember thinking, *This can't be normal,* but I'd just tell myself that it was nerves and would pass. It wasn't nerves. Luckily for me, he was a pretty conservative guy when it came to physical stuff, and I never even had to tell him that I didn't want to have sex with him. We had a lot of fun together, but when it finally became clear to me that we were just friends, I drove to his house and broke up with him. That night, I went out to celebrate my break-up with a bunch of my social-work classmates!

Now I will fast-forward to my junior year of college and the infamous Rome study-abroad trip, which was pretty much the drop of water that burst open my gay floodgates. I had a good friend named Kelly on the trip, who was out and proud at the time. She was the only lesbian friend I had back then, and I wanted so badly to confide to her some of the "possibly gay thoughts" that were swirling in my head. I'm pretty sure she knew I was gay as soon as I said, "Hey! You know what would be fun? We should make out sometime. Just for fun, you know? I've always been curious about what it would be like to kiss a girl." Yeah, I wasn't fooling anyone. Eventually, we ended up in an Irish pub in Rome, drank a beer or two, and started holding hands under the table. As soon as my friend Nichole got up to go to the bathroom, our conversation went something like this:

> Kelly: "Hey, Chelsea, have you ever kissed a girl before?"
> Me: "No."
> Kelly: "Do you want to?"
> Me: "Yes!"
> Kelly: "Do you want me to kiss you?"
> Me: "Okay!"
> (Kiss happens)
> Kelly: "How was that?"
> Me: "Awesome."
> Kelly: "Better than kissing a guy, huh?"
> Me: "Way better!"
> Nichole comes out of the bathroom, and end scene.

Yes, Kelly was a good friend to me. I'm sorry to say that I was pretty distant and awkward around her for a while after that, though. It was just part of my process, but taking that first step of admitting to myself that I really was attracted to women was a scary one. For a while, I told myself that I was bisexual, because it was easier to think that I might still have a chance at a "normal" and "acceptable" relationship in the eyes of society. I am by no means implying that bisexuality is a phase on the way to accepting your gayness. In fact, bisexuality is probably much more common that heterosexuality or homosexuality,[1] and I will not deny that I have definitely felt physical attractions toward men at times in my life. However, it stops at that level for me. Once I try to think of anything physical happening with a guy, the attraction mysteriously vanishes.

It was a long time before I was actually able to say the words "I'm a lesbian" out loud to myself. Even then, I was alone in my living room, and I practically had to force the words out of my mouth. When I finally did it, I started crying, and all I could see ahead of me was a dark, unknown future full of fear and rejection. All I could think was that I would never have a family, I would never have kids, my family was going to hate me, and I was going to lose all of my friends. Fortunately for me, not one of these things was or is true. I still do not have a family or children of my own, but if I decide that this is what I want someday, there will be nothing to stop me from living any life I dream of living. The future may look a little different for me now than I imagined it as a kid, but I have since learned that being gay has nothing to do with whether or not I can live a happy and fulfilling life.

Getting to that point wasn't easy. It took several years of soul-searching and really getting to know myself before I truly became comfortable in my own skin. I always knew logically that there was nothing wrong with being gay and that I shouldn't have to hide it from people, but I didn't feel that way in my gut for a long time. Once I was finally able to download that unconditional self-love from my head to my heart, though, it was the most liberating epiphany of my life. The key to achieving this is just to "fake it till you make it." Keep thinking the same positive thoughts over and over again until they become a belief, and your new belief will download into your heart when you least expect it. One day, you will have your own story to share about how you came out to yourself. When that day comes, you will be able to look back on your fears and smile, because they will no longer have power over you.

Chapter 2

The Many Gifts of Being Gay

Being gay is not a curse or an affliction, but one of the greatest gifts we could ever have been given. By choosing to come out and accept yourself for who you really are, you are taking your first steps on a journey toward transforming your life forever. It will change from one of fear, anxiety, shame, or doubt to a life of unconditional, unbounded self-love and joy.

Gayness is like Miracle-Gro for your soul. It causes you to grow stronger and more quickly than you ever would have otherwise. Being gay will teach you so many amazing things, some of which you may already have experienced in your own life. It will teach you to become more accepting, open-minded, and non-judgmental. You will also become a critical thinker, while developing a solid understanding of what your beliefs are and why you believe them, unlike many people, who primarily believe something because a person of influence told them to believe it (religious leaders, parents, teachers, role models, etc.)

One of the most important lessons you will learn is how to truly love yourself and become independent of the opinions of other people. Just as crucial as mastering self-love is learning to genuinely forgive and love when other people have said or done hurtful things to you. If you have not realized it already, you will come to discover that you do not forgive to heal other people; you forgive to heal yourself. Anger and resentment will destroy you, and forgiveness is the only way to set yourself free.

Each of these incredibly valuable skills is essential to being able to live a truly happy life, but until they are forced to come face to face with a challenging situation like coming out, most people have the luxury of choosing not to think about them. Of course, everyone has the opportunity to work on forgiveness, becoming critical thinkers and being open-minded, accepting, and unconditionally loving of themselves and others, but when you're gay, you don't have any other option. It's sink or swim. We have to make a choice to learn these skills and thrive or remain in a prison of fear and darkness, never knowing the simple joy of being able to just be ourselves in the world.

Gay people are confronted with this truth at a much earlier age than most, but no matter what age you decide to come out, it is never too late to start this amazing journey. The wisdom you gain from it will be with you forever.

Chapter 3

Common Fears and Expectations

It cannot be overstated that the coming-out experiences of the millions of gay people worldwide are as diverse as the people themselves. However, there seem to be some universal themes and fears that most of us have to face at some point. Below are a few of the most commonly mentioned fears encountered by LGBT people during the beginning stages of their coming-out journeys.

People will treat me differently, even though I'm the same person I always was.

When people come out, especially to the people who are most important to them, a common statement of self-defense is, "I'm still the same person I was a minute ago, before I came out to you." It is definitely scary to think that people might not treat you the same way after you come out to them. Sometimes people do act awkwardly or differently around someone who has just come out to them. They may not know what to say to you or how to react, especially if you are the first gay person they have ever known personally; if they really care about you, the last thing they would want to do is say something that would cause you to feel even more vulnerable than you already do. Typically, this uncomfortable behavior only lasts until that person realizes you have not changed at all; then they feel they are able to relate to you again. The only change is that you have told them about one aspect of yourself that they were not aware of before.

Even though it might seem like other people need constant reminders of this fact, sometimes we need to remind *ourselves* that we are the same person as well. Many gay people think they have to change the way they look or act when they come out, in order to fit in with the gay community. If coming out inspires you to rock a new look or haircut or try out some new activities you've always held yourself back from, go for it! Coming out often gives people the courage and freedom to express themselves in ways they never dared to before, when they were trying very hard to conform to societal norms. Remember, the gay community is as diverse as the human race, and no matter who you are or what your interests are, you are just as gay as anyone else. All you have to do is be yourself.

My family and friends won't love me anymore.

The fear that your family and friends will disown you is one of the biggest fears people have when coming out. It is a possibility, and it does happen to people. However, as our society continues to make progress toward acceptance and equality for LGBT people,[1] more and more people are coming out and demonstrating that the fears of homophobic people[2] in our country and throughout the world are groundless. Every day, people are coming out to their families and adding positive stories of unconditional love to our rich history. I have listened to many people tell their coming-out stories over the years, and I have never met one person yet who has had more negative responses than positive ones. In the end, you will simply be left with the people in your life who love you completely and without condition. Everyone else will either come around eventually or remove themselves—and their judgment—from your life.

I could get fired from my job.

In our country today, there are only twenty-one states and the District of Columbia that currently have state non-discrimination laws for gay and lesbian people. Four of those twenty-one states do not include protections for gender identity and expression.[3] Many people are unaware that it is still legal for an employee to be fired from his or her job simply for being gay. This makes coming out at work a real concern, especially if you live in one of the other twenty-nine states without any workplace protections.

When you are just beginning the interview process for a new job, be sure to take a look at each company's employee nondiscrimination policy, to see if it includes sexual orientation or gender identity. If it does not, you may want to ask one of the current employees about the culture of the company and how inclusive and sensitive it is to the needs of LGBT employees. At any rate, try to find a company that values being open and accepting of all of its employees; otherwise, you could be setting yourself up for a lot of frustration and negativity in your work environment. You have enough to worry about at work without the added distraction and worry that you will be fired just for putting a picture of your partner on your desk.

For those who are already employed and have a desire to come out at work, take the same first step by checking your company's employee nondiscrimination policy. If you have worked at this particular job for any length of time, you have probably been able to gauge the general presence or absence of homophobia that exists there. In a safe environment, it would probably be okay to simply come out to someone by dropping some details of your life into a conversation over lunch about your weekend. Pinpoint a few people you trust, and see how they react to you. Then you can ask their opinion of whether or not it would be a good idea to come out to the rest of your coworkers. As in any other situation, who you decide to come out to is completely up to you, but be smart about it. If you really think your job could be put at risk, make sure you have a backup plan, an emergency "rainy-day fund" in place, and the ability to support yourself financially until you find a new place to work, preferably one with an LGBT-inclusive nondiscrimination policy.

Everyone will see me through a "gay lens."

In the beginning stages of coming out to other people, it is common for a person to feel self-conscious around others who know they're gay. They may be afraid that they will now be seen as gay first and "John" second. I have often heard people in conversations refer to their "gay friend" so-and-so, making that person's sexual orientation the primary focus of their being. Although people are often seen as the "token gay" in a setting in which they are the only out LGBT person, others are often only as aware of your sexual orientation as you are. The more self-consciously aware you are of the fact that you are gay, the more you will be inclined to bring attention to it. This is not to say that being gay is something you need to keep to yourself, but the more comfortable you become in your own skin, the more other people will begin to see *you,* and not just the gay person who is you. Also, once you have been out for a while, your gay identity and everything related to it will no longer constantly be at the forefront of your mind, the way it is when you are first coming out. As a natural result of this, the fact that you're gay will just not come up as often as it seems to in the beginning.

Although it might seem counterintuitive, when we first come out, often *we* are the ones seeing *ourselves* through a gay lens. Without realizing it, so many people view themselves based on a self-image that was given to them by someone else. This is not unique to LGBT people, but so often in our lives, we have heard things about the LGBT community from other people and unconsciously absorbed them as part of our self-image. These are what I like to call blind self-images, or B.S., because they blind us to, or can severely impede, our view of who we really are: beautiful beings of light and love. Here are a few examples of B.S. as it relates to the gay community:

Gay people aren't good parents." B.S.

"Gay people aren't capable of having long-term, committed relationships." B.S.

"Being gay is a choice." B.S.

"Jesus said that being gay is a sin." B.S.

"If you're gay, you can't have kids." B.S.

"Gay people are bad or perverted." B.S.

"Gay people are all very polite and well-dressed." B.S.

That last example is usually true, but not always. Seriously, though, once you start to become more aware of the internalized homophobia and unconscious thought patterns that have been ingrained in you for a lifetime, the gay lens you have been seeing yourself through will begin to disappear. One day, being gay will be acknowledged as just one awesome aspect of what makes you who you are, instead of taking center stage as your primary identity.

There aren't any other gay people like me.

A lot of people who begin to question their sexuality often think, *I couldn't be gay, because I know how gay people are. I'm not like that.* Let's be real. There are a lot of stereotypes about the gay community, and straight people are not the only ones who buy into them. Of course, it has to be said that stereotypes of any group exist for a reason, and there are certainly many common characteristics that gay men often share and others that lesbians often share. However, pop culture has a lot to do with how gay people are portrayed in society, and many people, including gay people, get all of their information about what it means to be gay from watching movie and TV characters.

It is not uncommon for someone to feel like they have to change their look or behavior once they come out in order to "be more gay," whether that means chopping off their hair, pretending to like activities that others expect them to like, or dressing a certain way. Being an invisible minority, people often do these things in an effort to make themselves more visible to other gay people. But then you have to ask yourself the question, "What does a gay person look like?" Gay people come in all shapes, colors, and sizes and can be found in every race, culture, religion, and vocation. We also come with every type of clothing and hairstyle, so just be yourself. The best thing about being part of such a wonderfully rich and diverse community is that there are no rules! You can be anyone you want to be, and there will never be any other gay person quite like you. As Judy Garland said, "Always be a first-rate version of yourself and not a second-rate version of someone else."

One of the reasons why it takes so much courage and strength of character to come out is because there are so many unknowns to account for. It is absolutely human to have fears about the future, but one of the best ways to normalize and alleviate those fears is by talking to other people who have been there and come out the other side. You are not alone in your uncertainties, but once you finally get past the initial stages of coming out these unknowns will no longer exist; your old fears will be long gone.

Chapter 4

Gender Identity and Expression

In our society, there are a lot of labels, stereotypes, and "correct" ways of being that are assigned to pretty much every culture and subculture of people under the sun. Of course, this is no different for the LGBTQ community, and gay people often buy into stereotypes about the gay community just as much as straight people do, regardless of whether or not these stereotypes apply to them.

As I mentioned previously, when someone is first coming out, they may often feel pressured to change their appearance or behavior to fit into certain stereotypes they have heard about what it means to be gay or lesbian. Whatever the reason, though, the fact is *there is no wrong way to be gay.*

Many of the general stereotypes about gay and lesbian men and women are based more on gender expression than sexual orientation. While it is true that stereotypes often have some truth to them, many people believe that all gay men are feminine, love fashion, and dig Broadway show tunes, while all lesbians are masculine, have short hair, and are experts in the use of power tools. Personally, I am a show-tune-loving lesbian with long hair (currently), who loves playing softball and using power tools! Seriously, though, the fact is, there are plenty of feminine straight men, as well as masculine straight women. On the flip side, there are lots of masculine gay men and an abundance of feminine gay women. The same goes for people who identify as bi or trans; and of course, there are many gay men who have a more feminine gender expression and lesbian women with a more masculine gender expression. If you look at sexual orientation and gender identity/expression on a bell-curve spectrum, most people probably fall somewhere in the middle. The main point is that sexual orientation and gender identity/expression are two separate concepts, and the way you choose to express your gender is just one more liberating way to be your unique and special self.

One of the greatest things about the LGBTQ community is how incredibly diverse it is. It is one of the only minority groups that includes every kind of human being in the world. Gay people can be found in every country, culture, and ethnicity on earth, which means we are all very different, but we are all still gay! In my younger, more ignorant days, I often thought to myself, *I can't be a lesbian, because I'm not butch. There are no other gay people like me out there. I'm "too normal" to be gay.* Guess what? There is no such thing as normal. There is only an infinite number of beautiful expressions and possibilities of human beings' potential to be themselves. Take every opportunity to express yourself authentically, because when you are true to who you really are, you will attract similar people into your life.

Chapter 5

There Is No Wrong Way to Come Out

Just as there is no wrong way to be gay, there is no wrong way to come out. However, there may be some methods or strategies that are more effective than others, which will be discussed in a later chapter. This book is entitled *A Coming-Out Guide,* but this may be a bit of a misnomer. Typically, when you think of a guidebook, it teaches you step by step how to do something, meaning that there is a right way and a wrong way to do it. So, of course, the guide is meant to help you figure out the right way to do it, so you don't end up trying to dry your clothes in your washing machine, for example. However, when it comes to coming out, there is no one "right way" to do it. In fact, there are an infinite number of ways to come out, because there are an infinite number of ways for individuals to express themselves.

We are all different, and we all have different levels of comfort and different paces at which we do things. Gay people, as a community, are the most diverse subgroup there is, because any and every type of human being on the planet has the potential of being born gay. We come from all cultures, age groups, genders, races; you name it, there is a gay version of it. Even though there may be endless ways of coming out, there are also many common experiences that gay people share on their individual coming-out journeys, which gay people can almost universally relate to. That being said, the purpose of this guide is to show you several possible strategies for coming out that might resonate with you, thereby providing a starting place for you to find your own way and develop your own unique coming-out story.

"Coming out" means different things to different people. For some people, coming out may just mean coming out to themselves. They might feel completely content just being able to sit with themselves and finally say, "Yes, I'm gay, and I'm okay with that." They may not feel it necessary to tell anyone else, now or ever, as long as they can just revel in the relief of being able to be themselves *with* themselves. Many people find peace of mind that way. There are other people who finally realize they are gay and want to go out and tell the whole world! They are proud of it and do not feel any qualms about letting people know. As the saying goes, "I'm here, I'm queer, get used to it!"

Most people fall somewhere between these two extremes, and coming out is a much more gradual process. The two previous examples could also be incorporated into a person's coming-out journey as a beginning, an end, or one of the steps along the way. Someone may come out to him- or herself and then wait a long time before coming out to anybody else. They may come out to a family member first, a close friend, or a person whom they are not very close to at all. It could be a mixture of all of these. Many people have the surprising experience of having their family tell them that they are gay before they have even realized it for themselves! It's different for everyone, and there is no specific timeline that you need to be on or specific order in which things should be done. It's all up to you and what you feel comfortable with. Everyone has their own individual coming-out story, and you should always do what works best for you. Give yourself permission to move at your own pace, because the essential thing is that you feel happy and at peace with where you are. If you feel a lot of inner turmoil because you are not out to certain people and fear is the primary factor holding you back, consider taking baby steps.

Building Up Your Self-Love Support System

One of the safest and most effective ways many people have found to take the first steps on their coming-out journeys is to start by telling the people who are most likely to be accepting and supportive. This is extremely helpful for a few reasons:

1. It sets you up for success, because this greatly increases the likelihood that your first coming-out experiences will be positive. Before coming out, one of the primary fears many people have is that no one will love and accept them for who they are. If you allow yourself to come out first to people who will not only accept you but be thrilled about it, you will immediately prove this fear to be false in your own mind.

2. It gradually builds up your confidence by allowing you to experience what it feels like when another person is excited and happy that you are finally allowing yourself to be who you are. Receiving this reaction from other people gives you permission to feel the same way. Often, gay people feel embarrassed or guilty when they begin coming out to people, because they have had it drilled into their heads that being gay is something to be ashamed of. The more times you see people responding positively to your news, the more you will come to believe within yourself that coming out is a happy and joyful thing. It is also true that your expectations of how a person will react to you often influence the reaction you receive from them. If you expect someone to react badly, you may be less likely to deliver your coming-out news in a way that portrays it as something positive; you may even cause the other person to think of your coming out as a bad thing, because they can see that you are not happy about it yourself. On the other hand, if you are positive, confident, and self-assured in your presentation, people will be more likely to see your news as a good thing for you, because they can see how happy it makes you to be honest about who you are.

3. It will also give you practice for coming out later in situations that may cause you more anxiety, such as coming out to family members and close friends. Once you start your coming-out journey, you will continue to come out to people for the rest of your

life. Even when you are completely out of the closet and comfortable in your own skin, you will always be coming out to new people. Like anything else, the more you do it, the easier it gets. You will also begin to develop a feel for how and when to come out to different types of people in various situations, but the best way to start is by practicing in a safe environment with people who love you no matter what. Think of these awesome people as your coming-out training wheels!

Chances are, you can immediately think of at least one person to bring into your self-love support system. As a gay person, it is often very noticeable when someone makes a gay-friendly remark, especially if it's something you're not used to hearing. Those people often stand out in our minds as a safe space, because we know that if we so choose, we can be ourselves around them without having to worry about an awkward or tense situation developing out of judgment or ignorance. Once you have taken the time to build up a strong support group to share in your joys and help you through the harder times, fear will begin to lose its hold on you. You will begin to build up the courage to come out to the more intimidating people in your life, because you will have the self-assurance that there are people who will love you and have your back, no matter what other people's reactions might be.

If it isn't fear that's holding you back from coming out to other people and you genuinely just don't care if others know your sexual-orientation status, then who cares what anyone else thinks? You *do not* have to tell anyone you do not want to tell. It's all about how you feel on the inside and finding inner peace. If you are able to obtain inner peace from only being out to yourself, great! On the other hand, if fear *is* the main thing holding you back from coming out, and you're feeling a lot of inner conflict or anxiety about the fact that you are not out, then you probably should come out eventually. You just need to get your support system in place and find the right time and environment that works for you.

Most importantly, never let anyone make you feel pressured to come out in any given situation or feel like you are not a "good enough gay person" if you don't tell the whole world right away. You should never have to feel guilty about whether or not you decide to come out to someone. I've had a few straight friends whose friend or family member came out to them, and they told me things like, "I feel kind of offended (or sad) that they didn't come out to me earlier. How could they think that I would judge them for being gay?" Suddenly, the coming-out event becomes all about *them* instead of their gay friend or cousin. Of course, this does not mean that these are bad or selfish people; they just want you to know that they love you.

If you come out to someone who reacts this way, it may be because they don't understand that you have to come out when *you* are ready. It's a personal choice, and it has nothing to do with how much you love them or whether you respect them enough to tell them first. In fact, the most important people in a gay person's life are often some of the last people to find out that their loved one is gay, because they care more about those people's reactions than anyone else's. It is devastating to think you might lose them.

People have very legitimate reasons for the timing of their decision to come out to specific people. If you are in high school and are fairly certain that your parents would react badly to your coming out to them, it may be very wise to postpone that conversation until you are out of the house and in a position to support yourself more independently. You never want to risk putting yourself in a position of having to support yourself before you are ready. It certainly does not mean that you don't love them, but it may not be in your best interest at the time. You are the only person who can be the judge of that. If you are sure your parents are not going to kick you out of the house for being gay and you want to come out to them, by all means, go for it. That's great! The sooner you tell anyone, the sooner that person can begin the journey of acceptance and understanding that you started such a long time before.

A college professor gave me some very insightful advice about coming out to my mom. She said to think of your own coming-out process as a train leaving a station. When you come out to your parent or anyone else, their train is just pulling out, and you are way ahead of them. You have to be patient and realize that they need some time to catch up to where you are in your own understanding, just like you needed when you first came out to yourself. This is assuming, of course, that the person you are coming out to does not already know you're gay. Many times, people will surprise you by saying, "Oh, I've known you were gay for a long time. I just wanted to wait for you to tell me."

The basic message here is that there is no wrong way to come out, and you should never let anyone pressure you into coming out. You get to be in charge of who you come out to, when you come out to them, and how you come out to them. Always be sure that you feel safe, and remember that there will be a learning curve for most people. Try to make yourself available to answer their questions, without getting too defensive if the questions seem ignorant. Everyone is ignorant about something until a patient and caring person takes the time to educate them. If you are gay, you are a teacher; there is no way around it. The good news is that all you have to do to teach and inspire others is to simply and unapologetically be yourself. You will be amazed at the number of people who will learn and grow from knowing you.

Chapter 6

Unconditional Self-Love

When we are born, regardless of where, there are some essential things we must have, in order to grow and develop properly: food, water, shelter, clothing, and love. The first four are obvious, but love may not be the first thing most people think of as a basic survival need. However, without love, a baby quickly learns that there is no one there to care for it and meet its needs. It may lose its will to cry when it's hungry or thirsty, because it has learned that no one will come. Without love and care, the baby may begin to develop psychologically damaging emotional beliefs and chemical patterns in its brain, which can affect its ability to function successfully in the world.[1] We come from love and are created by love; human beings cannot survive without it.

There are, of course, many different ways to express your love for other people and many ways to receive it. The expression of a person's love differs for friends, romantic partners, and family members. Although the expression of love may take different forms, the love is all the same, and babies are the greatest experts on loving. Babies don't judge people; they just love unconditionally, because that is all they know how to do. As they grow, however, the world begins to teach them that there are certain people they should fear.

At first, this fear usually comes directly from their parents' beliefs about the world, and later, as they grow, they begin to form their own beliefs, based on personal experiences. They learn that they can't love everyone unconditionally because they will get hurt. Although some of this is healthy fear— such as learning to avoid danger or being taken advantage of—people often become afraid to love others because of previous emotional trauma. Unfortunately, this emotional trauma often creates an internal belief that they themselves are unlovable. This is the challenge that must be overcome, because it's impossible to truly love other people until you are able to love yourself.

Coming out is the ultimate expression of self-love. Just by picking up this book, you are already on the right track, because you are proving your willingness to begin the journey of unlearning the lessons of judgment and self-hate that the world has taught you. Learning to love yourself really isn't about learning anything new. It's about *remembering* the only truth you knew when you came into this world: you are whole and perfect just the way you are. Self-love means embracing who you really are and living your truth, no matter what other people may say or think about it. Self-love also means you must always honor where you are right now, and you should never let anyone—yourself included—force you to take steps on your coming-out journey that you are not yet ready to take.

When you love yourself unconditionally, you are honest with yourself about your feelings, and you observe those feelings without judgment. Choosing not to come out to your parents before you're ready, for example, is just as powerful an act of self-love as joyfully proclaiming your gayness to the world at the Pride Festival or marching for equality down the streets of Washington, D.C. Coming out is an act of courage, and it takes time to overcome some of the ingrained negative beliefs about being gay that we have all grown up with in this society. The only way to move past these beliefs is to love yourself through them. When you begin to truly love who you are, the old voices in your head begin to fade away because their words no longer ring true. Those old ideas and beliefs become laughable and silly. Eventually you begin to wonder how you could have ever bought into any negative talk that you heard growing up about gay being bad.

Thinking negative or unloving thoughts about yourself is nothing more than a habit, and a habit is nothing more than the same thought repeated over and over again until it becomes chemically hardwired into a belief.[2] So many people have fallen into the habit of believing that they are not good enough or that they should be ashamed of who they are. The great news is that all you have to do to change these damaging beliefs into positive ones is think positive thoughts about yourself over and over again until the new thoughts become new beliefs to replace the old ones. The even better news is that you don't have to believe your new, positive thoughts for this to work. How could you believe them? They haven't become a habit yet! I'm sure that most people have heard the saying, "Fake it till you make it." This is a great mantra for a journey toward unconditional self-love.

Another name for these self-loving thoughts and positive self-talk is "affirmation." An affirmation is just a positive phrase that you think, write, or say out loud to yourself, that you want to be true in your life.[3] Writing down your own affirmations and saying them out loud to yourself every day can be very powerful. Another beneficial way to practice this is by writing affirmations on your bathroom mirror with a washable marker, so that you can look at yourself while you're saying them. Some examples of affirmations specific to gay and lesbian people could be:

"I am strong and brave. I have the power to overcome any challenge, and no one can hold me back."

"The potential and possibilities for my future are endless."

"No matter what society says, I can and will live my own truth. I will be happy, no matter what."

"My future is bright and full of joy."

"I am perfect and loved just the way I am. I don't need to change a thing. I love every part of me."

"Because I am gay, I am stronger. Because I am gay, I am wiser. Because I am gay, I have gained the courage to live my truth. Because I am gay, I have learned to forgive. Because I am gay, I have become a critical thinker. Because I am gay, I have become more accepting of others. Because I am gay, I have learned to truly love myself."

There are an infinite number of affirmations you can create for yourself, but the important thing to remember is that these do not have to be things that are true for you now. They can also be things you *wish* to be true, thoughts that you genuinely want to believe about yourself and your life. If you continue to repeat positive affirmations like these to yourself every day, several times a day, you will begin to believe them. Then your life will begin to transform from one of negativity and a focus on limitations to a life full of love and endless possibilities. This is when the real fun begins, because you start to see events and people show up in your life to reinforce the new, positive thought patterns you've created. Your new beliefs about yourself will become stronger than ever.

Unlearning old thought processes is a process in itself, so try extra hard not to judge yourself or feel guilty if some ingrained negative thoughts pop up now and then. Just remember that you were not the one who put those thoughts and beliefs in your head, and you do not own them. All you have to do in these situations is remind yourself that you come from love, you love yourself, and love can never be flawed. It is your true essence.

It's helpful for some people to wear a necklace, bracelet, or some other type of symbol to remind them to treat themselves kindly and think loving thoughts toward themselves. Below are some examples of the many wonderful ways to practice being kind to yourself:

- eating healthy food, getting enough sleep, and exercising
- taking special time to do what you want and need to do for your soul and not letting anything interrupt it or come ahead of it

- meditating
- getting a massage
- reading a good book
- spending time before you fall asleep at night telling yourself some of the things you love most about yourself

Aside from these more concrete actions, I mentioned earlier that self-love is perfectly expressed by honoring your present feelings and being willing to meet yourself where you are. In this sense, acts of self-love could take the form of:

- finally admitting to yourself that you are gay or lesbian and that it's okay
- choosing to come out to important family members and friends when *you* feel ready, *not* when other people think you should
- expressing your gender identity in the way that feels most natural to you and not worrying what other people think about it
- allowing yourself to be out in some environments and closeted in others, according to your own comfort level, so that you feel safe
- surrounding yourself with a loving support system of people who encourage you to grow and be yourself
- giving yourself permission to say no to attending family gatherings or other events that make you feel anxious, uncomfortable, or unsafe, including LGBTQ events, like pride festivals and equality rallies, if you're not ready for that kind of thing yet

- feeling free to practice religion or walk away from it; your spirituality has nothing to do with other people's opinions of it
- getting rid of every excuse for why you can't live the life you dream of living

This list could go on and on, and you may have already thought of a few things to add to it. If you have, congratulations! You are beginning to train your heart and mind to focus on love instead of guilt, shame, and judgment. If you haven't, this is a great list to get you started. I encourage everyone to make their own self-love action list right away and make it a priority to put at least one thing on the list into practice every day.

Other than the attainment of inner peace, another very important reason to learn self-love is that this is the only way to truly love other people and have healthy, happy relationships. When you see the beauty in yourself and realize how truly wonderful and unique you are, you begin to recognize these same qualities in the people around you. The same is true for people who focus on the things they want to "fix" or "change" about themselves. Have you ever noticed that people tend to point out the qualities in others that they themselves feel most insecure about? This is why many people who bully gay or gender-diverse people turn out to be gay themselves. When you truly love who you are, you stop focusing on "faults" and start seeing the good in others. The great thing is that other people start to turn their focus on your gifts and beautiful qualities as well.

It is important to clarify that self-love and arrogance are two very different things. Arrogant people only see what they perceive to be the shortcomings of others and believe that their way of being is the "best way." True self-love realizes that everyone has their own personal truth, and we are all unique expressions of love in the world. No one is better or worse than anyone else. We are all wonderful.

Chapter 7

Forgiveness

Although forgiveness is certainly something all human beings grapple with, gay people are provided with opportunities to practice forgiveness on a daily basis. It is especially crucial to realize that this is probably the most important—and possibly the most challenging—thing an LGBT person needs to learn in order to lead a happy and healthy life. You may have heard the quote by St. Augustine that says, "Resentment is like taking poison and waiting for the other person to die." No one speaking honestly would ever say that it feels good when another person denies who they are, treats them as less than an equal, makes insulting comments, or, in the worst case, physically harms them out of fear and prejudice. We're humans, not robots. Anger, frustration, and sadness are completely normal emotional reactions to these types of experiences, but if you ever want to be able to live a happy life, it cannot be accomplished without forgiveness.

Have you ever tried to be angry and feel good at the same time? It's impossible. The truth is, when you feel hurt by something that someone has said or done, that person often may not care whether you forgive them for it. In fact, they may not even feel that their actions need forgiving. As long as you choose to hold on to those feelings of resentment, the only person left hurting is you.

Think of a person who makes you angry. Maybe it's a parent or friend you've recently come out to, who thinks you're just "going through a phase" or someone who is verbally or physically bullying you at school or work. Maybe you're feeling frustrated with yourself for the way you responded to a situation in which you had to decide to be yourself around someone or stay in the closet. In all of these situations, choosing to forgive the other person's actions may not change that person at all. They might not even know you are forgiving them, but when you choose to forgive someone else, you change yourself. Holding on to anger only keeps you trapped in anger. When you forgive someone, you set yourself free because you are reclaiming control of your own emotions. Forgiveness means that you are taking back any power you have given away to other people and refusing to let them have control over how you feel about yourself and your life. So don't forgive other people based on whether or not you think they deserve to be forgiven. Forgive other people because *you* deserve to forgive them, because you are worth it, and because you deserve to live a happy, joy-filled life. Refuse to give others the power to bring you down.

The definition of true forgiveness is letting go of the anger and hurt feelings you have toward a person because of something they did, and replacing them with a genuine feeling of gratitude for the lessons you learned and growth you gained because of that person's actions. Be thankful for the people who cause you the most pain, because they are your greatest teachers. It may seem unfair or even wrong to give these particular people so much credit, but without them, you would never grow to your full potential. When you exercise, you cannot build up your muscles without resistance. It's not just preferable but absolutely necessary for your muscles to get torn up a little bit before they can grow back stronger; it is exactly the same with growing in wisdom and strength of character. Of course, you can learn good life lessons from unconditionally loving and respectful friends and family members, but the biggest growth experiences always come from the people and events that cause us to overcome adversity and find a way to be happy despite what we've been through.

Coming out is one of the defining growth experiences in any gay person's life, partially due to the fact that so many people are willing to teach you that you don't have to believe everything people tell you. Every time someone tells you you're not good enough, it is an opportunity to practice self-love. It is so much easier to forgive someone immediately when you feel gratitude for the amazing gift they are unwittingly helping you achieve. It is hard to master anything without practice, especially self-love, and every prejudiced, or even hateful, person who comes your way is just helping you get better and better at it. This does not just apply to being gay either. Whenever people are being judgmental or making fun of you about your weight, race, job, disability, or any other reason, that is your chance to own your awesomeness and send silent gratitude to that person for helping you love yourself that much more.

Although there are plenty of prejudiced people in the world to help us learn these lessons, it is important to recognize that most of our opportunities to practice forgiveness will likely come from people who unwittingly say hurtful comments to us out of honest ignorance. In these situations, learning forgiveness is synonymous with learning patience. Be patient with the people who love you, and help them catch up to where you are in your understanding of what it means to be gay. This shows a compassionate maturity that will only bring others into a closer relationship with you and cause them to grow as well. However, this can only be achieved by developing the conscious awareness that comes from intentionally growing in unconditional love for yourself.

Without these people, we might never learn forgiveness. Everyone can continue to grow throughout their lives without facing too many hardships or obstacles, but the plants that grow to be the healthiest and most vibrant are the ones that get the most shit dumped on them in the beginning of their life. So forgive and be grateful for all of the adversity and challenging people you encounter throughout your life, because you will be stronger and blossom more intensely than you ever would have without them.

Chapter 8

The Only Tools You Need

When you choose to come out, what you are really doing is choosing to live your life in love, instead of living in fear. When I first truly experienced self-love, it was nothing I was able to force myself to do. I had been making a conscious effort to change my thoughts, but self-love was not something I could "download" from my logical mind to my heart. I knew it was important for me to really feel it and believe it in my heart, but I didn't know how. Luckily for me and everyone else in the world, you don't have to know *how*. You just have to want it. I knew I wanted to truly love who I was, and one day it just hit me. The download from my mind to my heart was finally complete.

In *A Course in Miracles,* it says that "miracles occur naturally as expressions of love. The real miracle is the love that inspires them. In this sense, everything that comes from love is a miracle."[1] When you are finally able to really love yourself, it is a miracle, because it is coming from love. The same is true of forgiveness. Forgiving somebody is an act of love for yourself, because forgiveness is always for you. It is not for the other person, because you are the one who is set free from anger and hurt when you choose to forgive someone else. So being able to forgive is a miracle too.

A Course in Miracles also says, "Miracles are habits and should be involuntary. They should not be under conscious control. Consciously selected miracles can be misguided."[2] Basically, if you have the intention to forgive, you don't have to try. At some point, it will just happen. This is the experience I had when I was finally able to forgive one of my family members for the many hurtful things he had said to me in the past. It wasn't a consciously selected action. One day, when I was driving from Fort Worth to Austin, it just happened without any effort. I suddenly felt an overwhelming sense of gratitude and compassion for this person, for all the life lessons I had learned from him and the ways I had grown from those experiences. I realized that he was unable to love others in a healthy way because he had never experienced that kind of healthy, unconditional love himself. I also felt such compassion for him that day, because I realized that even if I could forgive him and release myself from all of that emotional pain, he can never leave himself. It is up to him to change his own thoughts and beliefs about himself and forgive himself for all of the hurt he has caused in his own life. No one can do that for him, and he will never truly be able to love other people until he learns to love himself. All the anger I'd ever felt toward him vanished in that moment, because I knew he had taught me forgiveness, which is one of the greatest gifts I have ever received.

We have all had someone in our lives we needed to forgive. Whether or not we have been able to forgive those people will determine the extent to which we are free to move out of the past and into a joyful future. *The Course* also says, "Miracles are always affirmations of rebirth, which seem to go back, but really go forward. They undo the past in the present, and thus release the future."[3] That is what self-love does and what forgiveness does. Self-love and forgiveness set you free. When you are forgiving someone, it may seem like you're going back and digging up the past, but what you are really doing is freeing yourself to move forward into the future, letting go of all the hatred, pain, anger, and hurt that have been holding you back from experiencing true happiness in your life. With self-love and forgiveness, you can accomplish anything; they are the only tools you need.

Chapter 9

Coming Out to Yourself

Despite the incredible diversity of the LGBT community throughout the world, there is one aspect of all of our coming-out journeys that we will always have in common: we all take our first step by coming out to ourselves. It is a bit ironic that coming out to yourself is the only situation in which you will not have to say or do anything at all, and yet *you* may be the hardest and scariest person you ever come out to. Times are changing, and we have made huge strides toward positive acceptance of gay people as a culture in the United States over the past few decades.[1] However, being able to recognize and accept that you are gay in the current world can be terrifying. For some people, admitting they are gay would be the equivalent of throwing away the future that they—and often their family—had always dreamed they would have. For others, it can be completely liberating, but for most people, there is some combination of relief and fear about their new, unknown future.

Coming out to yourself is a very individual experience, and everyone comes to realize in different ways that they are gay.

It is also true that everyone has a unique emotional reaction to accepting that they are gay. Often, people experience a grief reaction to coming out, grieving the loss of their old identity and the future they think they are losing, as well as anticipating the possible loss of important relationships in their lives.

The following are some common examples of how people may experience Elizabeth Kübler-Ross's five stages of grief, from her book *On Death and Dying,*[2] as it relates to coming out to themselves. I have included a sixth stage, guilt, which is a very typical emotion in most people's coming-out process, especially if they have grown up as part of a conservative religious community. Depending on a person's cultural background, spiritual history, and family situation, they may experience all or none of these stages. If coming out to yourself is taking the form of a mourning process, it is important to remember that there is no wrong way to grieve. Most people will go back and forth between these various stages before finally reaching a level of acceptance and comfort with the fact that they are gay.

Different Stages of Self-Acceptance

Denial:

- "*I* can't be gay! I wasn't raised that way."
- "I'm nothing like *those* people."
- "I just haven't found the right guy/girl yet."

It is not uncommon for someone to go in and out of denial during the beginning of their coming-out process. Some people remain in denial for years and never admit to themselves that they're gay until after they have gotten married and had children. One of the cutest and funniest denial stories I have heard came from a Christian friend of mine. She was always very involved in her church community, and her faith in God was and is still very important to her. Before she realized she was gay, she remembers feeling the Holy Spirit very strongly around certain close girlfriends of hers. Eventually, she realized that the "holy spirit" she was feeling was a strong dose of love hormones.

Anger:

- "This isn't fair! Why did *I* have to be born gay?"
- "I was supposed to have a family with kids someday, and now I'll never be able to."
- "So now I don't get to have equal rights? I'm just as good as anyone else!"

Before coming out to other people, it can be easy to lash out angrily at others for little things that normally wouldn't bother you. It is extremely painful to walk around with anxiety, fear, and anger about being gay, especially when you have no one to talk to about it. Obviously, you want and need to get those feelings out for your own health, but misplaced anger toward your loved ones will only serve to alienate them from you before you have even given them a chance to react to your news.

Guilt:

- "I know that I'm attracted to women/men, but I've always been taught that it's sinful and wrong."

- "My family is going to think I'm gross and perverted."
- "Everyone's going to think this is something I chose."
- "What if my friends feel uncomfortable hugging me or think that I 'like' them just because I'm gay?"
- "My parents are going to blame themselves."
- "My grandma will keel over on the spot, and it will be all my fault!"

Being gay is nothing to feel guilty or ashamed of, any more than you should feel guilty for having blue eyes, being tall, or having curly hair. Homosexuality is completely natural[3] and can be found among every species of the Animal Kingdom[4]. Like left-handedness, homosexuality is much less common than heterosexuality but just as normal and healthy. If you are struggling with guilt or uncertainty over the moral implications of engaging in homosexual activity instilled by the Judeo-Christian perspective, there are resources listed in the back of this book that discuss what the Bible really says about homosexuality.

Bargaining:

- "Maybe my family and friends would accept the fact that I'm gay, as long as I don't talk about it around them and keep that part of my life to myself."
- "I know that I'm attracted to people of my same gender, but I'm willing to go to therapy if I could change."
- "Maybe if two people of the same sex fall in love and live together, but they don't have sex, it wouldn't be a sin."

In this stage, a person has begun to accept the fact that they are attracted to the same sex, but they are still looking for a way to change it or find a loophole, in which having such a relationship would be socially or religiously acceptable. Some people are encouraged by their families or church communities to try reparative therapies or participate in ex-gay ministries to turn them straight. However, these types of programs and therapies do not change a person's sexual orientation, only their behaviors.[5] In fact, they are extremely damaging to a person's self-esteem and do nothing but more deeply ingrain the idea that people with same-sex attractions are in need of "fixing." Reparative therapies do not work, because there is nothing to repair.[6]

Depression:

- "My life as I know it is over."
- "Nothing will ever be the same again."
- "My family and friends aren't going to love me anymore."
- "I'll never be able to have a family."
- "There are no other gay people like me."
- "I'm going to become a second-class citizen without equal rights."
- "My religion says I'm going to hell."

When you are going through a state of depression, it is crucial to find someone that you can talk to and confide in. If you are not yet ready to tell a close friend or family member what you're going through, try to find a supportive counselor, teacher, coworker, or classmate with whom you can share your fears. Finding even one other gay person who can relate to what you are feeling can make a world of difference. Hotlines like the Trevor Project are available every hour of the day to provide a safe space for anyone who needs a caring ear to listen to and comfort them.[7] Try to remember that fear and sadness, although excruciating at times, are a completely normal part of the coming-out process for most people. Though these feelings will certainly pass, you should never have to go through it alone.

Acceptance:

- "I know that being gay is not something that I can or must change about myself. It is just part of who I am."
- "I can still have a family after all. It will just look a little different than I always pictured it would."
- "Even though I still have a lot of fears about coming out to the important people in my life, at least I can now be honest with myself."

Once a person is finally able to accept the fact that they are gay or lesbian, they can finally begin to heal from all of the homophobia they have been indoctrinated with by society throughout their life. At this point in the process, a person may know logically that there is nothing wrong with being gay, but it may still take a lot of self-love work and conscious rewiring of old, negative thought patterns before this self-acceptance is downloaded into their heart.

This is certainly one process and set of emotions that a person can experience when coming out, and it is a very common one. However, there are other people who feel a great sense of relief when they finally figure out that they're gay. Finally, so many things about their feelings, friendships, romantic relationships, and childhood experiences begin to make sense to them. They may have felt like they never belonged anywhere or that they were always the "different" one, even within their own family. A person's discovery that they're gay can bring a huge sense of peace to their life. At last, they are able to experience the feeling of being part of a community where they fit in, where being "different" is the norm.

Acknowledging that you're gay is like giving yourself a permission slip to express yourself however you want, regardless of whether or not it breaks gender norms. Coming out to yourself is absolutely liberating, even in the midst of the fears most people have in the beginning, because it is such a relief to finally be able to just be yourself with *yourself*. If there is anyone in the world you should be able to be yourself around *without judgment*, it's *you!*

Chapter 10

Internalized Homophobia

Often when we are first coming out, one of our greatest fears is that other people will judge us. Unfortunately, for many people, their biggest critic is themselves. When it comes to being gay, this self-judgment is called "internalized homophobia," and it is the opposite of unconditional self-love. It is a belief that has been ingrained in your subconscious mind, which says you are inherently flawed just by virtue of the fact that you're gay. It is the voice inside your head that says, "Being gay is not okay, and everyone knows it."

This is not a belief that we are born with. It is something we are taught, both by the explicit comments we have heard from homophobic people in the world around us and by the messages we have been absorbing from the media and society our entire lives. Until recently, you never saw gay couples in TV commercials or in advertisements at department stores. Before Ellen DeGeneres came out on her sitcom, gay people were barely ever even seen on TV, let alone in a positive light.

When Ellen's show was canceled, that sent another message to the world that it is not okay to be gay.

Whether we like it or not, every one of us grew up in the same society, where, until very recently, messages that gay is a good thing were few and far between. When I was little, I remember hearing the words *lesbian* and *queer*. I didn't know what they meant, but I knew they were bad words. Most of us have grown up with the word *gay* being used as the ultimate insult or being used as a substitute word for *stupid, boring, weird,* or any other negative word you can think of, not to mention all the other words referring to gay and lesbian people that have been used as insults: *fag, dyke, queer,* and *homo,* to name a few.

Despite the traditional uses of these words, many of them have been reclaimed by the gay community over the past few years to have positive meaning. No gay pride parade would be complete these days without a "Dykes on Bikes" contingent, and I personally love to sport my "Homo-cyclist" T-shirt when I'm training for a long-distance bike ride. The negative use of the word *gay* has also decreased, as people have become more educated and aware of what they are actually saying.

The word *queer* is now very commonly used as an all-inclusive umbrella term in the LGBT community. In addition to LGBT people, it encompasses everyone who falls outside of society's traditional gender and sexuality norms but who may not necessarily identify as gay, lesbian, bisexual, or transgender. Also, let's face it, when you are referring to the entire LGBTQIAA community, "queer" is a lot easier to say than "lesbian, gay, bisexual, transgender, queer, questioning, intersex, androgynous, and asexual," but that is why we are called the "alphabet soup" people! It is important to point out that although it has been reclaimed, the use of the word *queer* within the gay community is still somewhat controversial and can be a loaded term for a lot of people. Using "queer" or identifying as queer is definitely a matter of personal preference, so it is probably better never to assume that a person feels comfortable being referred to as queer until you ask or hear them use it themselves.

Despite the fact that many of these terms have been reclaimed and many people are becoming more educated and aware of the way they use the term *gay,* all of us have had certain negative messages ingrained in our brains when it comes to what it means to be gay. Being gay does not make us immune to brainwashing, and there are many negative beliefs that we have to recognize, overcome, and change if we are ever going to truly experience unconditional self-love.

Gregory Herek describes internalized homophobia as some degree of negative feeling that LGB people direct toward themselves when they begin to recognize their homosexuality or bisexuality, having "internalize[d] society's ideology of sex and gender at an early age."[1] Another definition states that "internalized homophobia refers to negative stereotypes, beliefs, stigma, and prejudice about homosexuality and LGBT people that a person with same-sex attraction turns inward on themselves, whether or not they identify as LGBT," and "also applies to conscious or unconscious behaviors which a person feels the need to promote or conform to cultural expectations of heteronormativity."[2] Internalized homophobia is something every gay person deals with, and it is nothing to feel guilty about. It is just something you need to become aware of, so you can eventually stop it in its tracks and replace it with positive self-talk.

Remember that a belief is just the habit of thinking the same thoughts over and over again. We did not necessarily get to choose our beliefs as children, but as adults, we only need to become aware of our negative thought patterns and simply decide to choose new ones that reflect the place of unconditional self-love we want to reach one day.

Internalized homophobia can express itself in many different ways. It often comes in the form of anxiety, such as not wanting to hang out with other gay people because others might think that you are gay too; not wanting to hold hands with a date or significant other in public because you are afraid of people staring at or judging you; feeling insulted and defensive when a friend or family member asks you if you are gay or lesbian; leaving out parts of your life when catching up with friends or family because you assume that they will not accept you; or choosing not to talk about the person you are dating (even though everyone else is talking about their significant others) because you have decided that it would make everyone uncomfortable.

Even making the assumption that other people will not accept us for being gay is homophobic, because we are assuming that everyone else will automatically think it's wrong. It seems to be a common learned behavior among gay people to choose not to speak up for themselves when people are making gay jokes or homophobic comments; we come to believe that everyone else around us feels the same way as the person making the hurtful comments. It has become a conditioned response just to let it roll off us and act like it doesn't hurt. I have even caught myself not wanting to confront a friend on a homophobic comment or joke that they made because I don't want to make *them* feel uncomfortable or embarrassed. I would just think to myself, *They didn't mean anything bad by it* or *I know they're fine with me being gay and they love me. It would make them feel awful if they knew they insulted me.* The real truth is, if your friends really love you, they would never want to say things that are hurtful to you, and they would probably rather you call them on it and feel a little sheepish than continue to say something ignorant that unintentionally hurt your friendship.

The social trend in our country now is such that the majority of people are not okay with homophobic comments. So many gay people are coming out and being true to who they are, and you would be hard-pressed to find a straight person today who does not have at least one gay loved one in their life, whether that be a friend, family member, or coworker. Regardless of the negative beliefs about gay and lesbian people that someone may have grown up with, finding out that someone you love is gay forces you to question everything you have ever been taught. It is not such a black-and-white issue for society anymore, especially as more and more people learn that a person's sexual orientation is not something they choose but something they are born with.

Changing "But" to "And"

Sometimes when gay people talk about themselves, or when others refer to gay people, you will hear them say things like:

"I'm gay, *but* I'm a good person."
"He's gay, *but* he's really involved in his church."
"She's gay, *but* she's very pretty."
"He's gay, *but* he's an awesome quarterback."

This may not seem like that big of a deal, *but* it is. When you insert the word *but* after "I'm gay," what you are really doing is sending yourself and everyone else a subconscious message that being gay somehow makes you "less than" and that being gay is some sort of barrier you have to overcome, in order to do whatever you want or be whoever you want in life. Instead, try replacing "but" with "and," and notice how it completely changes the tone of what you're saying:

"I'm gay, and I'm a great person."
"I'm gay, and I'm an awesome football player."
"I'm gay, and I'm really involved in serving others through my church."
"I'm gay, and I'm beautiful."

Gay people hear negative language referring to being gay so often that it can be easy to internalize it and just take it. We become somewhat desensitized to it, because it almost seems natural for people to use *gay* as a bad word. The phrase "that's so gay" has been so commonly used as a substitute for describing anything negative that the people who use it often don't even realize that they're putting gay people down by saying it. When you live in a world that is constantly denigrating your identity in this way and immersing you in negative images of people like you, it can easily affect your self-esteem and self-image. It takes a tremendously courageous person to step back and say, "Those people are totally wrong! I know I'm a good person, no matter what anyone in my world may think, and I wouldn't change a thing about myself."

We all come into the world with that sassy self-love, but somewhere along the way, we are taught to forget it and replace it with other people's negative opinions. It is really sad how often we can hear ten amazing things about ourselves from other people and completely dismiss them, but the one time someone offers us a negative opinion or makes fun of us, we internalize it and carry it around with us for the rest of our lives. Unfortunately, some people have so many negative outside opinions floating around in their heads, they start to accept them as their own opinions of themselves. This is extremely damaging, not to mention the polar opposite of who they really are, which, of course, is whole, unflawed, and perfect love.

Making Your Self-Love List

A very powerful exercise I want you to try is to make a love list about yourself. Think of it as an affirmation to yourself that you can look at anytime, to remind yourself just how wonderful and uniquely special you are.

Step 1: Make your list.

Make a list of ten to twenty things you love about yourself. You can list physical attributes, talents, and special acts of love or kindness that you have done for someone else. For example:

"I love how I raised so much money for breast cancer research!"

"I love my smile."

"I love how I helped my grandmother by doing her grocery shopping."

"I love my gift for dancing!"

"I love how I helped that kid pick up all of his stuff when his bag broke in the hall at school."

"I love my sassy personality!"

"I love the kind way I took care of those stray kittens and found them all loving homes."

Most importantly, though, every list should include as number one, "I love that I'm gay! (Or lesbian! Or trans! Or queer! Choose whichever term you identify best with.) There is something very powerful about writing that and then being able to see it over and over throughout the day in your own handwriting.

Step 2: Make copies.

Post them all over your house, in your car, backpack, or purse, or on your desk at work. You could even take a washable marker and write your affirmation on the mirror in your room or bathroom.

Step 3: Read your list out loud.

Once you have made your list and posted copies of it everywhere, the third and most powerful step is reading your list out loud to yourself. Even if you do not believe how lovable you are at first, it becomes hard to deny the facts when you see and hear a list that constantly reminds you of what a true source of good you are in the world. *A Course in Miracles* says that every act of love is a miracle, and no miracle is greater than another.[3] All the lies you have been taught, that being gay makes you bad or less than anyone else, begin to vanish from your mind when it becomes constantly occupied with recognizing the truth of the loving spirit we were all born to be in the world.

So, go make your self-love list! Write it on the bathroom mirror. Put it in the places you look at the most throughout the day, and eventually you will start to see yourself the way the newborn baby version of yourself used to see you: totally in love with who you are and oblivious to other people's fears and judgments being projected onto you.

Chapter 11

Coming Out to Your Family

Whether biological, adoptive, or chosen, family is—or should be—one of the most important sources of love and support we have in our lives. Because of this, considering coming out to your family is usually one of the scariest and most daunting parts of the entire coming-out process for LGBT people, regardless of whether you are just now coming out to yourself or have been out for years.

As a minority group, the gay community has a very different experience from members of racial, ethnic, or religious minority groups, one or more of which you yourself may be a part of as well. The big difference for these other groups of people is that no matter how different, alone, or singled-out they might feel out in the world at large, at the end of the day, their family is just like them and is able to relate to their experience, with few exceptions. However, this is not usually the case for gay people. It can be very difficult and lonely, not only to feel different from everyone in the outside world, but also to feel like the odd person out in your own family.

It is certainly true that coming out is becoming more and more accepted and less shocking to people around the world every day. As gay people everywhere decide to be true to themselves and live open lives as the beautiful beings they are, their friends and relatives begin to realize that being gay is just as normal as being straight.

However, a fear many gay people have is that coming out will be the one thing their friends and family will not understand or accept, no matter how open-minded or liberal they may seem. A commonly expressed feeling of many heterosexual parents is, "I don't care if other people are gay, but *my* child isn't that way," or "Other people may be gay, but I didn't raise my child to live that kind of lifestyle."

Some people's belief system, which stems from their upbringing and often their religious background, is that homosexuality is a deviant, morally unacceptable, perhaps even "sinful" choice of lifestyle that goes against their religious community's beliefs. They have never been taught that everyone's sexuality is perfectly created by design. Therefore, for them to fully accept you would mean turning away from their faith and being forced to face judgment from their own peers. Your coming out signifies a coming out for them too, which includes their fear of the unknown reactions they will face.

Many parents have expectations from the time of your birth that someday you will get married and have kids for them to grandparent. The fear of losing their own future self-identity as a grandparent may be a disappointing and difficult pill for them to swallow, until they realize that gay people can still have both biological and adopted children of their own. When you come out to them, it may trigger a grief process or adjustment period, much like the process you may have experienced when you came out to yourself. During that time, it is important to assure them that you are the same person you've always been and that this is how you were born. Continue to remind them that you need their unconditional love and support, even as they take time to adjust to a new concept of you in their minds. Everyone learns and grows at their own pace, which is why patience and understanding are so important during this time of adjusting to your news. You have to remember that you have had much more time to discover and come to terms with your sexuality than your family has. Chances are, they will come around if you can try to make yourself available to answer their questions and help them understand you. This is all assuming, of course, that they do not already understand and accept it completely.

Coming out to your family may be one of the most anxiety-producing things you will ever do, but fortunately, positive coming-out experiences are happening more frequently all the time. Some people will completely surprise you. In my own life, I have learned never to count anyone out when it comes to learning acceptance and becoming educated about their gay friends and family members, no matter how stubbornly closed-minded, ignorant, or staunchly conservative they may seem. You may even have the experience of your family telling you that they have known you were gay for a while, and they just wanted you to be the one to decide when to tell them.

You just have to know that whether your family and friends accept you immediately or take time to come around, you will be okay. Nothing is more liberating for your soul than just being able to be who you are. Always monitoring which words you use, trying to remember who you have come out to, and carefully guarding your personal life is exhausting. However someone may react to your coming out, it is such a relief not to have to lie anymore or leave things out when people ask about your life. By the time we finally start coming out to other people, most of us have become absolute pros at using gender-neutral pronouns in conversations about our lives. I remember the lonely feeling I used to get when I couldn't share in the fun of talking to my family and friends about cool events I was involved in or people I was dating. For many gay people, once they finally come out to a loved one, they wish that they had done it sooner, to spare themselves the anticipation, anxiety, and fear they had during the time leading up to the actual event, especially if their fears later turn out to be unfounded.

Unfortunately, for some people, a positive coming-out experience is not their reality. They find that their family is not yet ready or educated enough to understand that being gay does not make someone any different than they were before they came out. In some situations, a parent may choose to ignore his or her child's professed sexual orientation or gender identity, preferring to believe that it is just a phase they are going through. In other instances, you may have constant arguments with your parents or find yourself constantly having to defend and explain to your family your experience as a gay person. As frustrating and infuriating as this can feel at times, you have to remember that your parents, friends, and other family members will all have their own process to go through on the way to accepting your news, just like you did. It's important for you to try to be as patient with them as you can.

If you are fairly certain that your parents or other family members will react negatively when you come out to them, there are several strategies for approaching the situation that can greatly improve your odds of having a positive experience:

- Bring a supportive friend or family member with you when you come out. Knowing that there is someone else in the room with you who has your back can help reduce some of the anxiety you will likely be feeling right before you come out to an important person in your life.

- Write a heartfelt letter, and read it out loud. Fear has a way of making us forget the well-thought-out speech we've been planning to present to our family, once the time finally arrives to come out to them. Writing it down and reading it to them in person allows you to say exactly what you want to say, regardless of the emotions you might be experiencing at the time. It is also helpful because you can give it to your family members afterward, for them to read again, as it is common for your news to come as a shock at first. Try to make the letter as personal as you can, so your loved ones can gain some understanding and insight into what you've been going through up to this point in your coming-out process.

- It is also extremely helpful to find a supportive adult mentor or family friend whose opinions and world view are respected by your family. Such a person is in a much better position to speak on your behalf, because they may know how to communicate with your family in a relatable way. It is also possible that your parents—or children, as the case may be—might be more open to being educated by someone their own age. If a person like this cannot be with you when you come out, you could suggest that your family members meet with that respected friend to talk about your news at a later time.

Ideally, one would hope that our relationships with our family and friends are such that we could have a conversation with them about anything, no matter how big a challenge it might be for us to find common ground and work through it. For some people, however, coming out to their parents or other family members in person is simply not an option. Others may choose to give their family a chance at having a face-to-face conversation about it, knowing that there is a real possibility of the situation becoming dangerous for them. How you decide to come out to your family—or not—is completely up to you, but your physical safety always takes priority over giving your family the opportunity to react well. If you genuinely believe that coming out to them could put you at risk, and you still want to go ahead with it, there are some precautionary steps that you should take to ensure that you set yourself up for the greatest success possible:

- You have the option of coming out from a distance, by making a phone call, writing a letter, or sending an e-mail. Being able to gauge your family's reaction to your news from afar will help you decide whether or not it would be wise to have an immediate discussion with them in person or wait awhile.

- The alternative, of course, would be to talk to your parents, family, or friend in person. In a potentially hostile situation, it's always a good idea to have an exit strategy planned if it becomes emotionally or physically unsafe for you to remain in your current environment. Have someone wait outside for you in the car if you think you may need to leave quickly afterward. If you are currently living with your parents, have a bag packed with fresh clothes, a toothbrush, important medications, and a list of phone numbers you could call or addresses to which you could go if you suddenly found yourself in a crisis situation.

- If being kicked out of the house is a real possibility, it is crucial that you are in a position to support yourself independently and financially before you come out to your parents. This primarily applies to young people or anyone who may still be living with their parents. There comes a time for most gay people when they simply cannot bear to stay in the closet any longer. Keeping such a huge secret can have a negative effect on your quality of life, as well as your physical and emotional health. If your circumstances are such that you feel you must come out to your family as soon as possible, *make sure you have a plan*. First find someone who will allow you to live with them for a while, or make arrangements to get your own place. Otherwise, you will be putting yourself in an extremely vulnerable position with nowhere to turn.

As much as we would like it to be, it is not always possible to control when people discover that we're gay. No matter how prepared they might be, some people will unavoidably find themselves in a state of unexpected crisis. Being told that you are no longer allowed to live in your own home may be one of the worst-case scenarios of coming out to your family, but it is a real possibility for many people. An article published by the National Coalition for the Homeless found that a disproportionate 20 to 40 percent of homeless American youth are LGBT,[1] despite the estimation that only about 10 percent of the youth population identifies as LGBT.[2]

Do not let yourself become part of these statistics. Whether you are an LGBT youth or adult, if you find yourself in crisis after coming out to your family, there are many people and organizations waiting to help you. The Trevor Project's Trevor Lifeline is a crisis hotline that is available twenty-four hours a day, seven days a week, for LGBT youth ages thirteen to twenty-four.[3] Lady Gaga's Born This Way Foundation website also offers many helpful phone numbers, hotlines, and information for finding LGBT resources for people of all ages in your area.[4] As scary as it might be to consider the possible negative reactions your family could have to your coming out, it is better to hope for the best and be prepared for the worst, so that if the worst-case scenario does happen, you will not have to endure the additional trauma of being out in the world with no plan or place to go.

In these hard times, it is very important for you to find loving support outside of your biological family and connect with people who accept *you*, not just their idea of what they think you should be. Many people in the gay community form what are called "chosen families." These are families of non-biological loved ones who fulfill the family role of unconditional love and support for one another and are every bit as important and legitimate as a biological family. Gay people also often find support from counselors, coming-out support groups, organizations like PFLAG and GSAs, open and affirming spiritual leaders, and teachers or professors. The important thing is to seek out someone who is going to empower you and remind you that you are perfect just the way you are.

No matter how a parent may react when you come out to them, almost 100 percent of the time, their reaction stems from the love they have for you and their present understanding of what it means to be a good parent. That is not to defend intolerance, bigotry, or verbally, emotionally, or physically threatening behavior in any way, but the fact is, most parents just want what's best for their kids. In most cases, parents and family members who react negatively to a relative coming out to them will come around eventually, out of love for that person. If you are in the position of having to come out to your own children, the most important thing they need from you is your love. The main desire any parent has for their child is for that child to be happy. Chances are, your children will want the same for you too.

Regardless of your family's response, you will have gotten one of the hardest parts of coming out over with. You will finally be able to experience the intense relief of not having to hide your true self from them anymore. There is nothing more freeing than being able to just be yourself. Courageously and genuinely loving yourself unconditionally for who you are is inspiring to all who witness it. When resistant families experience this authenticity and positive change in the way you live your life, they will have no choice but to eventually accept you completely too.

Chapter 12

Coming Out to My Family

My mom was the person I could talk to about anything. No matter what I brought to her, she was always there to laugh with me, soothe my fears or sadness, stay up late when I had too much homework, or give me advice on any subject. She was never judgmental and always knew the right thing to say.

For me, coming out to myself was a not a relief like it is for many people. It was simply a confirmation of the truth I had feared since the age of ten, and I felt like my life as I knew it was over. Keeping such a big secret was torturous, and every day I walked around with anxiety in my chest and a sunken feeling in my stomach. At a certain point, it became too much to bear on my own. I needed my mom.

Finally, I decided that I would come out to her over the holidays, while I was home from college. I had no idea how to tell her; I just knew that I had to, because I couldn't stand going through that pain and fear by myself any longer.

One day, I was sitting in the living room, pretending to study for the GRE, while hot tears streamed silently down my face. My mom saw me and invited me to come into her room to talk. She asked me what was wrong, but when I tried to speak, no words would come out. She took a few guesses before finally asking me if it was something to do with my sexuality. At that, I burst out crying and couldn't stop. At the time, I was pretty sure that I was gay, but I told my mom that I was bisexual. I thought that would be easier for her to hear because she could have some hope that I might be in a "normal" relationship one day. To my great surprise, my mom leaned over and gave me a hug. She told me that it would be all right and that I should just be open to everything and attached to nothing. She said she loved me no matter what. The emotions I felt were a mixture of shock, elation, and extreme relief. That could have gone down in history as the best coming out story ever—but that's not where the story ends.

You see, in my mind, I honestly thought that I'd come out to her, but, as I found out later, she hadn't understood what I was trying to tell her. In fact, there were a lot of things she didn't understand. My mom was brought up in a conservative Catholic family and had never even heard the topic of homosexuality discussed. Nevertheless, she was subconsciously taught by society that, although a person might be attracted to the same sex, it was not acceptable to choose a "gay lifestyle", nor was it the way God intended things to be. It had never occurred to her that a person's sexual orientation was pre-programmed before they were born. Her exposure to the gay community had been limited to news stories of gay pride parades on television and observing gay men coming out of night clubs. She didn't know that I had been struggling with fear and shame of being gay since age ten, or what I really meant to tell her that day: not that I was bisexual, but that I was coming to terms with the fact that I was gay, and I just hoped she would still love me.

About six months passed, and I was finishing my senior year of college. I had not brought up the subject of my sexuality to my mom again, and I had decided not to come out to any other family members for a while. All I wanted was some time to continue coping with my own feelings about what being gay meant for me and how I could get past my fears, in order to finally feel comfortable in my own skin. My one comfort was knowing that my mom still loved me and that I had her to help me get through it.

I had been accepted to graduate school shortly after coming out to my mom—or thinking that I had—and I was set to begin classes only two weeks after my undergraduate graduation. My family came to Austin to help me move into a new apartment, and it was during this move that I decided to tell my mom about a crush I had on one of my college girlfriends. She was the only person I had mentioned it to, and I was excited to share it with someone, until I saw her face. She looked at me blankly and asked, "What do you mean?"

I began to feel panicky. I responded with, "I thought we had already gone over this." Then she asked me, confusedly, "Are you telling me that you're gay?" As it turns out, she thought I was just going through a phase the entire time and that it had already passed. Much time had gone by since we first talked about this, and I had assumed she was fine with everything. On the contrary, she thought that everything was back to "normal".

Many questions followed, and although I know she was just trying to understand, some were so hurtful. "You're not going to tell your sisters, are you?" She wanted to know if I planned to "live the lifestyle" and said that no one else needed to know; it was nobody else's business. "Why would you want to embarrass your family like that?" In that instant, my world shattered. The most crucial support that I thought I had was gone.

Over the next few months, our phone conversations always seemed to end in arguments and hurtful words. I would try to answer my mom's questions, only to have her ask the same ones again the next time she called. She felt scared for my safety and worried about me being targeted for bullying or hate crimes. She said she couldn't understand why I would open myself up to such danger, and she tried very hard to talk me out of my "decision".

It's difficult to describe what it felt like to lose the support of the one person I had always turned to and to then have to turn around and support her through the biggest crisis of *my* life. I don't know what I would have done to get through this challenging period if I hadn't had a small group of close friends to love me through it. They were always there to hug me when I needed to cry and assured me that it would all turn out okay. The primary thing that kept my relationship with my mom intact during that time was her unfailing willingness to try to understand what I was going through, no matter how hard it was for her to accept it.

The cycle of arguments, tears, and apologies on both sides went on, until one day, there was a sudden shift. My mom called me on the phone to tell me that she was finally starting to feel more comfortable with the fact that I was gay and that she finally understood that it was the way God made me. It was a total change of direction, and I was understandably confused, until she explained that she had confided in our close family friend and life-long family doctor. He told my mom that being gay is completely natural and that homosexuality is common among animals as well. Many doctors and professionals he worked with were gay. For my mom, learning from a trusted medical doctor that being gay is not a choice, but simply a normal biological state of being, was the thing she needed in order to bring down the barrier to her understanding of what I was experiencing. Years of society's disapproval of homosexuality had taught her that living your life as a gay person was wrong and sinful; but, with this new perspective, she was able to embrace me just the way I was, without fear or shame.

That one conversation with the doctor completely transformed our relationship back to what it had been before I came out. One of the funniest phone calls I got from my mom after that was when she excitedly informed me, "Chelsea, guess what! You can have your own children someday! You can get artificially inseminated!" Of course, I already knew this, but I didn't want to say anything to spoil the moment.

Once my mom was truly on board with the fact that I was gay, I felt ready to begin coming out to the rest of my family. I finally had my mom's blessing to come out to my sisters, so I picked the easier one to start with. She has always been a pretty laid-back person, but I was still nervous. A friend of ours from high school had recently come out, and he was the talk of our small town at the time. I told my sister that I was "like him", and she thought I said that I "liked him". When I repeated myself, the realization came over her, and all she said was, "Really? That's kind of cool, Chels."

Breaking the news to my other sister was a little more challenging; there's a larger age gap between us, and I was terrified of losing the close relationship we had. When I started coming out, she was still in high school, and, as we were both busy with school and lived in different cities, we rarely had an opportunity to communicate with one another about our lives. During my short vacations between semesters, I would come home from college and often hear my sister use the expression "that's gay", as many high school kids did. At the time, I was constantly on high alert for any sign or signal that might indicate which family member would be safe to come out to next. Hearing my sister say that kind of thing made it easy to make the snap judgment that she was homophobic, and I decided I should wait longer before coming out to her.

What I didn't realize then, was that it had become so ingrained in the teen vernacular to use the word "gay" to mean "uncool" or "stupid", people usually didn't realize they were saying anything offensive about gay people at all, including my sister. I was also unaware that my sister had several out gay friends and had even dated someone who came out to her after they broke up. She turned out to be one of the most supportive people in his life when he was coming out, and they are still dear friends today; but I never knew this, because I was too afraid to talk to her about anything gay-related.

As I mentioned previously, your family knows you better than anyone, so it's not uncommon for them to figure out that you're gay before you come out to them. Years later, I found out that my sister had asked my mom if I was gay more than once, but my mom would usually answer, "Well, if she is, it wouldn't matter either way." This was very frustrating for my sister, because she was still at a point where she didn't really know what it meant to be gay, and no one was willing to answer her questions about it.

A few months after my sister's high school graduation, she came to visit me in Austin. I had decided that I wanted to come out to her in person, and this would be my last chance for a while. It's amazing how the universe conspires in your favor when you're taking a positive risk in your life.

The first night she was there, we went to see a musical comedy called *Altar Boys,* which just happened to have a lot of gay undertones. At a certain point, one of the characters even seems to be on the verge of coming out to the audience, when his confession turns out to be that he's a Catholic. After the play, my sister asked me to take her downtown to hang out in Austin's gay club district. I couldn't believe what I was hearing! It was a sign to me that everything was going to be okay, and I realized later that it was also a hint from my sister that she was fine with people being gay. One of the funniest comments I remember her making that night was how all the gay clubs smelled so good. "It smells just like Abercrombie, Chels!"

Later that night, I told her I needed to talk to her about something important. I was so scared, I almost started crying, and I said, "I want to tell you that I'm ... a Catholic." Humor through intense anxiety doesn't often translate well, but she got the idea. First, she kind of laughed, and then she started to cry. She told me that she loved me no matter what and didn't care. Then, she told me another fact about her high school experience that I didn't know. When she was a high school freshman, there was a gay boy at her school who was out and proud. One day, a group of kids beat him up in the bathroom to the point of severely injuring him. He was seen around the school on crutches for a long time after that, and my sister was concerned about something similar happening to me. I cried with her at that point and told her that everything would be fine. I couldn't have been more relieved, but that relief could have come much sooner had I been willing to take a chance on my sister's unconditional love for me. Nevertheless, I believe that everything happens as it should, and I wouldn't change a thing about that experience.

After this, coming out to the rest of my mom's family was pretty easy. The only exception was one particularly conservative uncle, with whom I sat through a three-hour, intensely anxiety-producing religious discussion about homosexuality. The next day, I broke out in a rash of hives that lasted eight months. However, when my mom told my grandparents that I was gay and mentioned the stress-induced rash, my granddad promptly instructed her to assure me, "Mary Jane, you tell Chelsea that she doesn't need to get hives over us!"

My dad and his family were another story. Although I was raised in a small Southern town, I never heard as many gay slurs as I did when visiting my family in upstate New York. Considering this, I was pretty sure my dad would react badly to me being gay. So I decided the best thing to do would be to write him the most heartfelt and loving letter I could and give it to him to read in person. When I handed him the letter, the only thing I asked was that he read the entire thing before he said anything to me about it. In the letter, I told him how scared I was to come out to him, and I hoped that he would still want to be in my life, because I loved him.

I have said before that you can never really know how someone will react to you when you come out to them. After reading my letter, my dad stood up, crossed the room, and gave me a hug. He said, "You're my daughter, and I love you no matter what. Nothing could ever make me stop loving you." That was probably the most shocking moment of my life. I still don't talk to my dad much about my personal life, because he has told me that he still thinks being gay is a sin, and he never asks me about it. Despite the rocky start, my mom is now the most accepting and loving person in the world when it comes to LGBT people—or anyone else, for that matter.

It just goes to show that, even though someone may react with resistance or choose not to accept it when you first come out to them, if you allow them time to adjust, they could become your greatest ally. My cousins in New York, who seemed to be the most homophobic, have turned out to be some of my most supportive allies as well. On the other hand, just because a family member says the right thing, it doesn't necessarily mean that they will be the most supportive person in your life. At least they are doing the best they can with the knowledge and coping skills that they have at the time.

Today, my mom is one of the most accepting and proud parents of any person I know. She's my greatest advocate and a strong supporter of the LGBT community as well. She has cheered at the gay pride parade—especially for the "Bears" — helped raise money for LGBT causes, supported the gay-rights movement, and never ceases to be there for me with endless unconditional love. My coming out story was far from easy, but there are no longer any secrets to hide; because of this, I have a closer relationship with my family than ever.

In my personal experience, when you come out to family members, there are several things you should explain that may help them gain a better understanding. Many people are ignorant to the fact that being gay is not a choice. They think you can simply make it go away, but it's how you were born. Helping them understand this is paramount. For many of us, being gay is a fact that we've had to come to terms with over a number of years, and, often, it's the last thing many people want to accept about themselves. The resistant family members you come out to need to be told how scary it can be for you to tell your loved ones you're gay, facing the fear that they may not accept you for who you are. It's painful to consider the idea of being rejected, hated, or shunned; if you explain these things to your loved ones, it may help them gain a deeper understanding of what you've endured up to this point, and they will be more likely to show you empathy and compassion.

Those who don't want to accept your sexual orientation will need time to adjust to a new concept of you in their mind. They may be in denial or grieving the loss of the person they knew you to be; they need you to assure them that you are still the same person you always were. They love you and more than likely just want what's best for you. Try to be patient and give them lots of time to come around. If you can have the courage to show them that you are living your truth and that being gay is a part of yourself that *is* best for you, they will eventually come to know it in their own hearts as well.

Chapter 13

Religion and Spirituality

Now we are going to discuss a subject that certainly affects all gay people, whether directly or indirectly: religion and spirituality. It is worth mentioning again that the LGBTQ community is the most diverse minority group in the world, and we are no less diverse when it comes to our beliefs about religion and spirituality, as well as the ways in which we choose to practice our spirituality, or whether to practice it at all. Whether people consider themselves to be religious, spiritual, atheist, agnostic, or whatever label they choose, everyone needs to have certain activities and sacred spaces in their lives that nurture their soul and spirit.

Religion and spirituality is often a taboo subject in the LGBT community. It is no secret that many LGBT people have been emotionally wounded and rejected by their families and faith communities because of the unloving messages taught by so many conservative religious leaders. Many conservative Christian traditions teach that a person will go to hell simply because they are gay, which they often teach is a choice and not a physical characteristic that a person is born with. The truth is that many conservative Christians, who make such judgments based on the Bible, are not knowledgeable about what the Bible really says about homosexuality. In a later chapter, you will be given some powerful tools and resources to present to people when you encounter these types of situations.

Even if you are not or have never been part of a conservative religious tradition, chances are, you've had to listen to someone's uneducated judgment of "the gay lifestyle." Many parents reject their gay children because of ingrained religious beliefs as well. So, to say the least, bringing up religion to gay people can often be a sore subject.

Taking all of this into account, people who consider themselves to be both gay *and* religious or spiritual can often feel caught between two worlds. On one hand, a lot of people are shunned by religious communities for being gay, and on the other hand, they can be ostracized by the gay community for being religious or spiritual. Despite the pain many people have experienced as a result of other people's religious beliefs, it is necessary to state that there is absolutely nothing wrong with religion, as long as it is being used as a tool for teaching people to love each other, instead of a divisive weapon to indoctrinate and control people's behaviors. At its best, religion provides people with positive inspiration and structured guidance on how to live their lives in a loving and meaningful way. Nowadays, there is an ever-increasing number of "open and affirming" religious communities that accept all people exactly as they are, and these faith communities have made it part of their mission to make LGBT people feel welcome.[1]

There are also many people who consider themselves to be spiritual but not religious. This is becoming more and more common in the world today, and there are many ways to practice spirituality outside of a traditionally religious setting.

A spiritual practice can be as simple as an activity that lifts your spirit, and yes, you can be atheist and still have a *spiritual* practice. Obviously, not everyone will be able to get their spiritual needs met in a religious setting, and it is crucial to find some kind of community that can uplift and inspire you on a regular basis. This could take the form of a weekly yoga group, meditation group, or hiking group. Some people get their daily or weekly dose of love, inner peace, and community from volunteering their time at an animal shelter or Habitat for Humanity. Exercising, sex, listening to good music, or reading an inspiring book can all be spiritual experiences as well.

Anything that makes your soul feel joy can be considered a spiritual activity, but whatever your spiritual beliefs are, the most important thing is to discover your personal truth and find a community to share it with. As important as it is to find a self-love support system, it is just as essential to have a group of people who share your specific spiritual beliefs. A *spiritual* support system is a group of people who can bring you back to inspiration when you forget how to inspire yourself. So whatever form it takes, make it your mission to find out what brings you joy and lifts your spirit. Make this spiritual practice a regular part of your weekly routine, and you will inevitably be stronger for it.

Chapter 14

My Spiritual Evolution

My spiritual journey as a gay person has been one of the most insightful, frightening, liberating, anxiety-provoking, and joyful adventures of my life so far. I love to look back now and then on some of things I've done and just laugh. As a high school kid, I would never in my wildest dreams have imagined myself standing up in front of a college Catholic congregation a few years later and making an announcement that, "The LGBT student group will be selling GBLTs (goat cheese, bacon, lettuce, and tomato sandwiches) and GAYtorade for a fundraiser after Mass!"

I was a "cradle Catholic," which means that I had been Catholic from the moment I was born, baptized as a baby, received my first Communion, got confirmed, and went to Mass every Sunday with my family. Both sides of my family were strongly Catholic, one side being southern Italian and the other side being German/Irish. I have to say that I enjoyed growing up in the Catholic Church, and I never really experienced the whole stereotypical "Catholic guilt" as a little kid. That part came later.

As they say, though, hindsight is 20/20. When I first began to think back on my little lesbian Catholic self, I started to recognize all the telltale signs that my family and I both chose to ignore at the time. For one thing, it was like pulling teeth to get me into that frilly, white dress at the age of nine for my first Communion. If you have never been Catholic, you may or may not know that at your first Communion, you receive the sacramental bread and wine for the first time during the church service, or Mass, in remembrance of Jesus' Last Supper before being crucified. It's a pretty formal occasion, and the typical dress for a little girl is a fancy white dress, a veil, and maybe some lacy gloves.

I wasn't having it. My mom finally made a compromise with me that if I wore the dress, I wouldn't have to wear the gloves or veil, but I could have a little flower wreath on my head instead. I reluctantly agreed. The metaphorical cherry on top was that I had a coach-pitch softball game right before the service, and I had to change into my dress in the car on the way to church, in order to get there on time.

Fast forward to my high-school years, just after my vest-and-polo-shirt phase and right before my overalls phase. Around ninth or tenth grade, most Catholics do something called getting confirmed, a ceremony in which you confirm your Christian faith as a young adult. Before getting confirmed, we were required to attend a Confirmation retreat, where we stayed in cabins in the woods and talked about Catholic stuff all weekend. I recently found an old journal that I was writing in at the time of this retreat, and I must have been in some serious denial not to realize I was totally gay back then. I was so innocently clueless. Here is an excerpt from my journal on the weekend of my Confirmation retreat. Observe how the passionate teen angst builds as the entry progresses. In the event that my friend should read this someday, all names have been changed to protect my ego:

4/06/2001

Sup homie journal?

> *I'm writing you from the top bunk of a cabin at my confirmation retreat camp. Guess what! My bunk had my name on it, and it was totally random! Lots of my friends are on this retreat. Kinda boring, but I bet it'll be better tomorrow. Too bad my friend Cindy couldn't come too. She is such a wonderful blessing to me. I can talk to her about anything, and I couldn't ask for a better friend. I never have to feel like she's going to judge me. I love her so much, and I'm going to miss her more than anything when we graduate. I hope we are always friends because I can't say that I know a better Christian person. She is such an incredible person with such a beautiful heart. I don't want to lose someone like that. I'm going to write to her as much as possible and visit her whenever I can. I know how lucky I am to have Cindy for a friend because I know that I could never find a sweeter, more loving, compassionate, and incredible friend in the whole world. I want to cry, but I just can't! Why? I don't know. I don't want to lose any of my friends, but most of all in the world I don't want to lose Cindy. She is the living expression of love. It just flows out of her and radiates to everyone like the sun. She's the beautiful smiling face that I can think of*

and get through anything. I love her soooooooooooo much
with all of my heart and mind and soul!

Now if that's not denial, I don't know what is. What I
did know for sure back then, though, was that I was a "good
Catholic girl," and good Catholic girls were *not* gay.

As I said before, I didn't truly come out to myself until
I was twenty-one, and it was never really my thing to spend
social time with church people, until I got to college. That
was when I discovered the Catholic Student Center at my
university. I made a lot of really close friends there, and it
was definitely the place where most of my personal growth
happened during my college years, because that was when
I first began to question all of the religious doctrine and
beliefs that I had been taught since birth. If you have always
been taught by religious leaders that being gay is a bad thing,
and then you realize that you yourself are gay, it brings into
question every other belief you've ever been taught by that
religion. It's also important for you to realize that when you
come out to your own family members, they will be faced with
the same challenge of whether or not to question their lifelong
beliefs and moral ideologies. When I first started questioning
my Catholic beliefs, I had to look up now and then, to make
sure that there wasn't a storm cloud swirling above me with
lightning waiting to strike me down. Eventually, I began to
realize that what I felt in my heart was the real truth, and I
began to have more of a personal relationship with God on
my own terms.

I spent the next year or so selectively coming out to friends
and a couple of family members, which was both terrifying

and a complete relief at the same time. Eventually, I decided that if I was going to remain involved with my community of friends at the Catholic Center, I had to come out. I was tired of constantly feeling like I had to hide the fact that I was gay, as if it made me less of a good person somehow. For me, it was all or nothing. I decided I would talk to my favorite priest about it, and if he told me I was going to hell, I would walk away and find a new community. To my surprise, he told me that there was nothing wrong with being gay and that he knew lots of gay priests. He even gave me some gay-friendly resources to give to my mom, to help her reconcile her Catholic beliefs with my sexuality.[1]

After that, I started coming out in full force, and I quickly became the token gay of the Catholic Center. It probably goes without saying that this was *not* always easy. I became very skilled at stuffing down my emotions around ignorant religious bigots and remaining outwardly calm while I explained my perspective on Catholic doctrine to them. One of the things that helped me the most during this time was that I made it a point to become thoroughly educated in what the Bible *really* says about homosexuality and what the actual Catholic Church teachings were.[2]

Humor also goes a long way in relieving painfully awkward situations. It was a surprise and a relief for me to discover that there were far more supportive people than homophobic people at the church. For a lot of my friends, I was the first out gay person they had ever met, and I was able to turn a lot of their negative beliefs and stereotypes about gay people upside down. No matter what someone's religious or personal beliefs are about gay people, once they discover that one of their loved ones is gay, it forces them to reconsider everything they were ever taught. In my experience, most of the time they completely change their point of view, if their point of view was even negative to begin with.

Even though I had many supportive straight friends at the Catholic Center during this time, the experience of being "the only one" in any setting can feel pretty lonely sometimes, and I began to realize that I needed more gay Catholics around me. This inspired me to begin one of the wildest projects of my life so far, creating an LGBTQ and straight ally student group at the Catholic Student Center. I talked to the same priest about my idea a couple of weeks after our previous conversation, and he told me that there was actually another priest there who would be interested in helping me get the group started! I couldn't believe my luck, until the other priest told me that we would need the bishop to approve it.

So I set out to come up with a proposal for a gay group that would be Catholic enough to convince a bishop, which was no small task. I was very nervous when I received an e-mail back from him, but to my surprise, the bishop told me that it sounded like a much-needed ministry, and he was happy to support it! Then he asked me what transgender meant. So I hit the reply button, thanked him, and began explaining what it means to be transgender. Teaching a Catholic bishop the definition of transgender is something I never would have imagined myself doing in a million years!

I named the group Prism. In the beginning, we were not quite sure how to go about finding people to join the group; so I painted a huge rainbow sign with a cross on it and hung it up in the atrium of the Catholic Center. Creating a loving and supportive environment was always the most important goal of the group. We made it clear that we would be discussing the teachings of the Catholic Church at times, but it was always up to each individual to take that for what it was and discover his or her own personal truth. Prism was just a safe space where people could be gay and Catholic without any judgment whatsoever. I'm happy to report that Prism is still alive and thriving today, after years of changing minds and hearts and giving gay Catholics a place to be themselves.

After all the time I spent at the Catholic Center and all the experiences that went along with establishing Prism, I began to realize that my spiritual beliefs had changed as much as I had. They had grown to be very different from what I knew to be fundamental Catholic beliefs; so much so that I knew that I needed to leave the Catholic faith and find a spiritual path that was more in line with what I now knew to be true for me in my life. Toward the end of my time at the Catholic Student Center, going to Mass began to feel almost spiritually toxic for me. I always had a sense of being conditionally loved there; it was okay to be gay, as long as I wasn't "living the lifestyle," which, in Catholic terms, meant that I can be gay, but I can never be in a same-sex relationship.

For a long time afterward, I didn't go to church or have any regular spiritual practice at all. I didn't miss religion or the idea that there was a certain set of rules I had to follow or else something bad would happen to me. Eventually, I really began to miss the community and support that I had received from all of my friends at church. There is something refreshing about having a positive place to go at least once a week to revitalize your spirit and enhance your emotional well-being. That was when I began to seek out other forms of spirituality and other faith communities. I started meditating from time to time, spending more time in nature, and making the time to read inspiring books. I also attended a Metropolitan Community Church (MCC) for a little while, which is a church that was founded specifically for LGBTQ people. As awesome as it was to see same-sex couples and out transgender people at church together, the MCC structure was still too religiously based for my new belief system. After a lot of soul searching and a little luck, I discovered the Unity Church, which has become my new spiritual home.

Like my coming-out journey, the evolution of my spirituality is an ongoing and inspiring process. The longer I live, the more I realize that the basic message of every religion and spiritual philosophy simply boils down to love. As long as you can figure out how best to live life in unconditional love for yourself and other people, it doesn't matter what faith you profess or what spiritual practice you use to get there. All that matters is that you are one day able to arrive at a place of living your life in love.

Chapter 15

Dealing with Bullying

I have already talked a lot about how important it is to have a support group or "chosen family" in your life. These are the people who will fill you with love, strength, and hope when you are running on empty. They are the people who provide a place in the world where you always fit in. When we're with these people, we don't have to modify our words or behaviors to make them feel comfortable, and we can just be ourselves, judgment-free.

This support can come from your own biological family, old friends, new friends, spiritual communities, or twelve-step groups. The important thing is that you find it. For some of us, this chosen family can mean the difference between life and death. It is a universal experience in the LGBTQ community to feel like the odd man out sometimes. Too many people feel like they don't fit in anywhere. They feel alone in the world, like they don't belong. They believe there is no one else like them and there never will be. Without people to remind you to hope and look toward the joy in your future, it can be easy to think that removing yourself from the world would be a better alternative to living a lonely life in a world that will never accept or understand you.

Bullying is unfortunately a very common experience that LGBT people face, not only as children and teenagers, but also as adults. It is often the result of other people's discomfort with those who do not conform to what society deems as "normal" (e.g., girls who feel more comfortable in boys' clothing, or boys who prefer ballet to football). Bullying can take many different forms. It is not always verbal or physical harassment, although those are the most visible and explicit examples. Sometimes bullying means intentionally excluding someone from a group because of a certain characteristic that person may have. Cyber-bullying is also a problem today, with people posting hurtful or threatening comments and messages through social media. If you have a coworker who is constantly making homophobic jokes or comments in your earshot that make it difficult for you to concentrate on your work and feel safe in your environment, that is bullying as well and could also be considered sexual harassment.

Bullying is a very serious problem, especially in schools, and it has to be stopped. If people don't feel emotionally and physically safe to be themselves at school, they cannot learn. LGBTQ youth have one of the highest school absentee rates of any minority group, and the suicide statistics among gay, lesbian, and transgender youth are staggering. Recent studies have shown that LGBT youth have rates of suicide attempts at least four times those of their heterosexual peers.[1] Just finding one person to talk to can make all the difference for a desperate person like this, and the most important thing they need to hear is that they are not alone.

If you are being bullied in school, the most important thing you can do is to let your parents, friends, and teachers know. Find a teacher or other adult in your school that you can trust, and go to them if you ever feel threatened or need to talk. If you feel comfortable telling your parents, this is even better. No one will be able to help you if they do not know what is going on, and you should never have to deal with bullying by yourself. Continuing to express who you are outwardly in spite of the way other people might treat you is extremely courageous and admirable, but always make sure that you have a plan to keep yourself safe. It is your school's absolute responsibility to create a safe environment for you to learn, and no one ever deserves to be victimized by bullying for any reason, especially for something as brave as being oneself.

There have been many efforts nationwide over the past few years to provide more support for LGBTQ students.[2] Many high schools, colleges, and some middle schools now offer clubs called gay/straight alliances (GSAs) or queer/straight alliances (QSAs), with a supportive faculty sponsor. Caring teachers and professors are wonderful people to confide in if you are in school and have no one to talk to among your family and friends. If you go to a school that does not have a GSA, there are resources in chapter 16 and in the resource section of this book to show you where to go to start one. The Trevor Project is another resource for you or anyone you know who may be having suicidal thoughts. This is a hotline that can be called any time, staffed by caring people who are always there to give you hope when you have none left.[3]

See the resource section at the back of this book for more information on resources and campaigns being implemented to create safe school environments for LGBT students.

Finding a good LGBTQ or LGBTQ-friendly counselor is always a great idea as well, if you can afford it and have one in your area. When I was first coming out in my early twenties, I joined a women's coming-out support group, and it was one of the best experiences of my life. Nothing feels quite as good as being able to work through your fears in a safe environment, where everyone else understands exactly how you feel. Many of these counseling centers base their fees on your income, so it can be very affordable or even free, particularly for students. LGBT community centers often offer free or sliding-scale counseling services as well. Seeking out counseling is always a good recommendation for anyone, but especially for people who find themselves thinking about suicide. There is always a way to work past a problem, and sometimes you just need a professional to help you figure out your own way.

When you are first coming out, finding a place to fit in or seeking out other people you can relate to can sometimes feel very frustrating or even impossible, especially if you are still in school or live in a small or rural town. Fortunately, it has become easier than ever to seek out other gay people or gay-friendly organizations. The Internet offers the opportunity to form an unlimited number of meet-up groups, where you can bring together lesbian hikers, a gay men's chess club, or a gender-queer soccer league. The sky's the limit! A group could even be created for people who are just coming out and need to find other people who are going through the same experience.

As a gay woman, I have certainly experienced bullying and discrimination. However, I would not change a thing about my life, because these are among the experiences that have caused me to grow in wisdom and strength. I would not be the same person I am today without those opportunities to grow and learn. I have heard well-meaning straight friends of mine say more than once that they would never want to have a gay child because of all the judgment and hardship the child may have to face in life. Being gay is not the problem; the problem is the ignorance and fear that causes the prejudice and hate to occur in the first place. Saying that it would be better for children to be born straight to avoid prejudice is no different than saying it would be better for all children to be born the same race, so that they would never experience racism. The diversity of the human race is what makes it so beautiful and interesting. Besides, if everyone was straight and of the same race, we would just find other characteristics to differentiate ourselves from one another. Being gay or gender-diverse is beautiful and perfect, and the more of us who are born to shine our light in the world, the safer and more accepting the world will become for us. So I tell my friends, do not wish for your child to be straight to avoid pain; wish for the world to become more loving.

You never have to be alone in the world. Go out and create your loving support system as soon as you can. Knowing you're not alone can give you courage and empowerment on your journey toward unconditional self-love. Then, one day, you will be able to provide that same love and guidance for someone else who is feeling lost, scared, and alone.

Chapter 16

"That's So Gay." Educating People and Standing Up for Yourself

Since the Stonewall riots officially marked the start of the gay-rights movement in 1969, there has been a great shift in US public opinion regarding equal rights for LGBT people. A Gallup Poll dated July 29, 2013 showed that 54 percent of the American public believe that gay marriages "should be recognized as valid, with the same rights as marriages between men and women," as compared to only 27 percent in 1996.[1] The progress that the gay community has made toward equality under the law over the last few decades is nothing short of incredible.[2]

Despite this inspiring cultural trend, it is still a common, often everyday experience for gay people to encounter homophobia through other people's use of gay slurs, homophobic jokes, and direct or indirect bullying at school, work, home, or within a faith community. The information in this chapter will equip you with several tools and strategies for standing up for yourself or someone else when a person says something uneducated or ignorant about being gay. This will not only be beneficial to whomever you are talking to, but it will help change the world one person at a time. These tools are proficient at exposing just how silly some of the comments and questions are that gay people hear constantly from uneducated people.

One of the most important things to learn about effectively conveying your experience to other people is this: it is not so much *what* you say to someone but *how* you say it. If you allow yourself to get outwardly angry, heated, and carried away by the ignorant things another person says, you have lost your opportunity to educate them and possibly change their mind. It has to be a conversation between you and the other person, not an argument. Otherwise you are just wasting your time. The difference between a conversation and an argument is that in a conversation, each person is listening to the other's point of view with an open mind, whereas in an argument, each person is too busy thinking about their next comeback to listen to anything the other person is expressing. Also, perceiving these types of confrontations as educated conversations, rather than arguments or debates, is much less intimidating, and you will probably have more confidence going into it with this frame of mind. In most cases, the more the other person can see that you are willing to hear them out and understand where they are coming from, the more likely they will be willing to do the same for you.

It is worth restating that there are no emotions that you "should" or "should not" feel when someone says something judgmental or hurtful to you. Feeling angry, offended, or hurt is a perfectly natural emotional reaction to a verbal attack. Nonetheless, you have to be able to rise above their unenlightened attitude and maintain your composure, despite your initial emotional reaction, if you want to have any chance of confronting them on their ignorance in a positive way. This is the only way to allow the possibility of successfully communicating your experience to someone and planting the seeds of change in their mind and heart. Martin Luther King, Jr. said, "Love is the only force capable of transforming an enemy to a friend." It may be hard and somewhat intimidating to have these conversations with a prejudiced person, but as with anything else, practice makes perfect. During my time at the college's Catholic center, I became an expert at having these conversations with a few religious "enthusiasts" I encountered there. The thing that helped me most was making sure I educated *myself* and that I was prepared and confident in my responses to their questions. It is always important to be as authentic as possible, and if you do not know the answer to a question that someone poses, just be honest and tell them. Sharing your personal story and experience is always more powerful and touching than trying to outsmart someone with "facts" that may or may not be accurate.

That being said, here are some great ways to combat ignorance and get other people thinking in a new way without ever losing your cool or breaking a sweat. One of the best tools is the "Heterosexual Questionnaire" by Martin Rochlin.[3] This questionnaire is fantastic, because it takes many of the questions and comments that straight people have been asking gay people for years and then flips the question around by replacing the word *homosexual* with *heterosexual*. This is a great technique for answering people's questions by directing their question right back at them, and it helps them to gain insight and a new understanding almost immediately. See Appendix B for a copy of Rochlin's questionnaire.

One of the most pervasive and perhaps most damaging phrases that has woven its way into the regular language of our society, especially that of teens and young adults, is "that's so gay," using the term *gay* as a substitute word for anything stupid or unpopular. To reverse this trend and bring awareness to people about the effect that their words can have on others, GLSEN and the Ad Council developed the Think before You Speak campaign in 2008. This campaign featured a series of funny public service announcements, where a celebrity would correct and educate teens who were using the phrase "that's so gay." These PSAs can be found at *www.thinkb4youspeak.com*. "Think before You Speak" suggests that you "turn it around" when someone says, "That's so gay." Use the offender's name or physical description in place of the word *gay,* to help them see how it feels (e.g., "That's so Jamie!" or in the words of Wanda Sykes, "That's so teenage boy with a cheesy mustache!"). This website also offers other helpful tools, such as guides for educators and information for parents of LGBT kids.[4]

There are many other positive pro-gay campaigns that have come out in the past few years to raise awareness, such as the "Legalize Gay"[5] and "Gay? Fine by me."[6] t-shirts, the "NOH8 Campaign,"[7] and the GLSEN "Safe Space" campaign.[8] The "Safe Space" campaign provides gay allies in schools with "safe space kits" containing two posters, a forty-two-page guide for educators on how to be an effective LGBT ally, and ten little rainbow triangle stickers that they can display somewhere in their home, office, classroom, etc., to show that they are a safe space for LGBT students and other adults. These kits can be ordered online at *http://safespace. glsen.org.*

Another fantastic tool for creating a safe school climate for LGBT students is to start a Gay-Straight Alliance (GSA) or Queer-Straight Alliance (QSA) at your school or university. GSAs are school clubs that bring straight and LGBT students together with the aim of providing a space for students to safely be themselves, regardless of gender identity/expression or sexual orientation.[9] If you would like to form a GSA at your school, visit *www.glsen.org/jumpstart* for all the information and resources you need to get started.

Whether we are youths or adults, one common situation that almost all of us have been in is defending ourselves against religious conservatives who believe that being gay is a sin. There are several resources available on how to educate others about the religious teachings of the Bible, specifically in regards to its teachings on homosexuality. One certain fact is that Jesus never once mentioned the subject in the entire New Testament. An excellent documentary on this topic is "For the Bible Tells Me So."[10] This film discusses all of the main passages in the Bible that have been used against LGBT people, as well as following the stories of five real people and their families on their journey of reconciling sexual orientation with spirituality. This could be a helpful tool to have friends or family members watch as well, if they are having a difficult time accepting your sexual orientation because of their own religious beliefs. Educating yourself on this subject is one of the very best ways to combat religious ignorance about homosexuality. For more excellent resources on this subject, see the resource section.

All of the tools and strategies presented here can be useful in changing the hearts and minds of the people in your world. However, you have to remember to be true to your own feelings at any given time. If you feel inspired to stand up to an ignorant person and try to have an educated conversation with them about your experience as a gay person, that is wonderful. If you are not yet at a level of comfort within yourself to do that, or you think that you may be putting yourself at risk, there is absolutely nothing wrong with ignoring someone or getting up and walking away from a negative situation. Deciding when and where to come out or stand up for yourself is always up to you; whatever choice brings you a sense of inner peace is the right one.

Chapter 17

Let's Talk about Sex, Gayby

Sex ... gay and lesbian style! It's not something we gay people are often taught in school or by our parents, but at least we know how the heterosexuals do it! We are pretty much left to fend for ourselves in that area, finding information where we can and hoping that it's accurate. Before the Internet, there weren't many places to get information on how to have sex if you're gay, let alone safe-sex practices. Basically, people had to figure it out based on trial and error, and hopefully you would eventually get the hang of it without picking up an STD. Nowadays, there are many books written on the subject of how to have great gay sex, and some reliable websites as well. If you don't feel comfortable walking into a bookstore and laying down your copy of *Gay Sex 101* at the cash register, you can always order any book you want on Amazon.com[1] or other bookstore websites.

The first time I got up the guts to buy a how-to book on girl sex, I marched into Barnes and Noble and picked up a copy of *The Lowdown on Going Down* by Marcy Michaels and Marie Desalle (which is actually a book written for heterosexual men, but there weren't too many other options that I knew of back then).[2] I tried to be discreet by buying it along with a copy of *The Hitchhiker's Guide to the Galaxy*[3] on top, but the cashier wasn't fooled. After I got over the initial nervous embarrassment and left the store, I learned a lot! To this day, I don't know why it never occurred to me to just order it online. However, this is not going to be a chapter on 365 days, 365 ways to have gay and lesbian sex. Plenty of people have covered that topic by now, so I'm going to talk about some of the important things people often don't talk about or know about gay and lesbian sex.

I want to preface this conversation by saying that we gay people are really lucky when it comes to sex, because we have a major advantage that straight people don't have, unless they are transgendered. Most men generally know what a man enjoys sexually without ever having had sex before; likewise, women know how their own bodies work better than any man ever could. That being said, even when we are about to have sex for the very first time, we come into it with valuable knowledge about what makes our own gender tick. Of course, everyone likes different things, and communication is the key to really great sex, but generally, gay people have a distinct advantage over heterosexual people in this area. So try to have a little compassion for straight people who go into the act of sex with very little knowledge of how the other person's body works or what they like, other than what they may have seen in a movie theater or on TV. Basically, when it comes to having awesome sex, being gay is a major plus, *and* you can have as much sex as you want without having one single pregnancy scare!

However, being immune to pregnancy does not get you a free pass out of practicing safe sex. One of the most common fears about sex for gay and lesbian people is contracting HIV/ AIDS or other STDs. If you do get an STD, many of them are treatable or can be cured, but you should immediately make an appointment to see your doctor if you ever begin to have symptoms that are out of the ordinary. Of course, it is always best to avoid getting STDs in the first place; you just have to be smart and educate yourself about them. Unfortunately, at this time in our country's history, LGBT people may be at greater risk for contracting STDs than their straight counterparts, due to the fact that most health programs in schools do not address safe-sex practices as they relate to LGBT people specifically.

A common myth in the lesbian community is that lesbians cannot contract STDs. It may seem like common sense to protect yourself by wearing a male or female condom, finger cot, or dental dam if you are having sex with someone with whom you're not in a monogamous, STD-free relationship, but in the heat of the moment, people do not always stop to think about it. Even if you do use protection, nothing is 100 percent foolproof.

This is why it's so important to find an opportunity to have a conversation with a potential sex partner about getting tested, if you think your relationship is moving in that direction. Of course, if you are mainly having one-night stands or hookups, you won't really have as much time to talk about this; but in that situation, you at least need to use protection. Never take someone's word for it that they are STD-free or a virgin. This is not to say that everyone you have sex with will be dishonest, but it is possible that they may have an STD and not know it. It's just not worth the risk to have unprotected sex if you or your partner have not had an STD test *recently*. If you are using protection, it's still not a bad idea to get tested first, just in case something goes wrong. It may be a little awkward or embarrassing sometimes to bring up the subject of STD testing, but it basically boils down to the fact that you need to love yourself enough to stay safe and healthy. Having that one conversation and taking the necessary precautions could mean the difference between life and death.

When you have been on at least a few dates with someone before considering having sex with them, it will be a little easier to broach the subject of safe sex, and it doesn't have to be a big deal. If you are mature enough to have sex with someone, you should be mature enough to have an adult conversation about it. You could bring it up by saying something like this: "It's obvious that there is some great chemistry between us, and if you want to talk about possibly taking our relationship to the next level, I have a few questions I'd like to ask you."

Then you could ask some basic things, such as:

- When was the last time you were tested for STDs?
- Would you be willing to get a blood test at some point before we have sex?
- If we decide that our relationship is not going to be monogamous, can we agree to always practice safe sex?

This may not be the sexiest conversation in the world to have with someone, but it's much better to have it in advance, rather than right before you're about to take your clothes off. It's easy to find a medical provider to give you a test, as most walk-in clinics can do it. Planned Parenthood is another good option for getting an STD test, and they are LGBT-friendly as well.[4] All you have to do is call the doctor's office or clinic and say, "Hi, I would like to schedule an appointment to come in for an STD test. What times do you have available?" Once you and your partner get it over with and find that you are STD-free, you can include sex in your relationship without a single worry about disease. If one of you does discover that they have an STD, you will be in a much better position to take the necessary precautions to keep both of you safe, as well as seek treatment for the existing STD.

When you go to the doctor for an STD test, it is not necessary to tell them over the phone that you have a same-sex partner, but once you arrive at the appointment, it could be a relevant subject to discuss with the doctor. There are certain health topics and questions that all LGBT people should discuss with their healthcare providers. A list of these health topics is available on the CDC website,[5] and there are specific links to this health information in the health resource section of this book. There will also be a link to a website where you can find a network of LGBT-friendly healthcare providers in your area.[6] Entrusting your physical well-being to a healthcare professional can feel vulnerable enough at times without the added stress and awkwardness that homophobia or transphobia can add to it. Many LGBT people do not get the basic healthcare they need because of the fear of coming out to their doctor or because of a bad experience they've had with a provider who was ignorant of the specific needs of an

LGBT patient. Knowing that your provider is LGBT-friendly and educated on LGBT issues going into the appointment will take a lot of the anxiety out of it and allow you to express your needs freely and without fear of judgment.

The bottom line is that when you are coming out and starting to date people you are actually attracted to for the first time, it can be easy to get carried away with the excitement of it. Sex is supposed to be fun, but it's important to be smart and stay safe. Having a slightly awkward conversation and taking intelligent and mature steps to stay healthy early on in a relationship will not only make the experience more enjoyable and worry-free later, but it could literally save your life. It all comes back to love for yourself and for your partner. Get tested. Then enjoy the ride!

Chapter 18

A Little Dating Advice

I would venture to say that many gay and lesbian people start learning about their self-identity, as it relates to their sexuality, by dating. However, this is not necessarily the most "cost-effective" way to go about it. When you start dating other people in order to get to know yourself, it can often be a big strain on both you and the other person.

When you start dating someone before you are ready to be in an "out," in-the-open relationship, some common issues will begin to crop up:

- You may feel anxious or embarrassed to hold hands with that person in public.
- You may feel the need to deny their existence to the friends or family members to whom you have not yet come out.
- You may feel pressured to go to certain LGBT establishments or participate in activities, events, or festivals hosted by the gay community, before you are

ready. Attending events like these before you are fully out can bring on the added stress of worrying about being seen by people you know and having them find out that you're gay before you are ready to tell them.

- You may also feel pressure to have sex or participate in certain sexual acts with the person you're dating before you feel comfortable or know what you want from the relationship.

The list could go on, but the point is that it's painful for both you and for the other person to have to feel like you can't act naturally with one another in public, just like any other couple would. It is also hurtful to keep hearing your significant other continually denying your existence or your relationship's existence to friends and family. Always introducing your significant other as your "friend" can feel pretty degrading for both of you, especially for your boyfriend/girlfriend/partner if they are more out than you are, because it completely devalues the real relationship you have with one another.

Of course, if you are dating or in a relationship with someone who is in the same place as you in that respect, the relationship is less likely to be negatively affected by the fact that neither of you is very out. Discuss the situations in which you both feel comfortable being out and natural about your relationship. This will probably enhance the relationship by taking a lot of pressure off of each of you, as you won't have to act comfortable being "out" in public when you really aren't. People often put themselves in an uncomfortable position, for fear of hurting the other person's feelings, but chances are, your date will sense your anxiety anyway. Honesty is always the best policy, because then you can pick an activity you'll both enjoy and inevitably have a better and more carefree time together.

A very viable alternative to help avoid much of this stress and anxiety is to get to know yourself by yourself first, *before* getting into a relationship. Getting to really know who you are and what you are looking for in a relationship before starting one gives you several advantages once you do start dating:

- You will feel more self-confident, because you have taken more time to get comfortable with the fact that you're gay. By this time, you have hopefully been rewiring old thought patterns into self-loving ones. You'll be less compelled to stress over what the other person will think of you and more inclined to just be yourself.

- You are better able to enjoy yourself when you are in public with your date, because you won't be so self-conscious about an awkward glance here and there or running into someone you know.

- You will also be more aware of the type of person you are looking to date, so you will be able to skip past a few "frogs" on the way to finding your prince or princess.

When I first came out, I didn't feel comfortable with dating, nor did I have any desire to date at the time. Dealing with the family drama surrounding my sexuality was more than enough for me to handle back then. I was often asked,

"How do you know that you're gay if you've never dated anyone of the same sex?"—to which I would always respond, "How did you know you were straight before you started dating?" Once I finally did start going out on dates with women, I certainly was not completely comfortable and carefree at first. One thing I can say with absolute confidence, though, is that the more "out" I have become, the more fun I have been able to have on dates and in relationships. It may sound strange to say, but it's a great day when you can just be upset about a breakup that lacked chemistry, like any other relationship, without there being some added gay-related layer of heartbreak, such as having to break up because your partner's family will never accept your relationship.

Once you are ready to begin dating, consider online dating sites, which provide many opportunities for making gay friends and meeting other gay people with similar interests. You can basically write out the recipe for your ideal girlfriend, boyfriend, "activity partner," or friend-with-benefits. One of the greatest things about online dating sites, from the gay perspective, is that you don't have to guess what someone's sexual orientation is! No more awkward, roundabout questioning to try to find out if someone has the potential to be into you. "So, hey, I think you're so smart and awesome and pretty, and by the way, would you happen to be gay as well?" (Awkward silence.) Not so with online dating! It's written right there on the screen. If you are an adult, you are looking to start tiptoeing into the dating world, and you have not yet tried online dating, you should at least give it a chance. It can be really fun, and it is also a great way to weed out a lot of deal-breakers before you ever even meet someone in person.

So, do yourself a favor and wait a little while after you have come out to yourself before you start dating. Once you have begun to care more about being loving to yourself and feeling good than about what the outside world thinks of you, you will be in a much better position mentally and emotionally to dip your toe into the dating pool.

Chapter 19

Advice from the Other Side of Things

The following are excerpts from the personal stories of a few LGBTQ people whom I have had the pleasure of interviewing. They made it through the initial stages of coming out and are all inspiring models of LGBTQ people living lives of openness, self-empowerment, and love for who they are. They have all gained wisdom and insight on their own coming-out journeys and welcome the opportunity to share their valuable advice with you from the other side of the closet door.

Age: 29
Gender: Female
Race: Hispanic
Ethnicity: Mexican American

I can describe my coming out in one word: liberating. I literally felt a weight lifting off my shoulders. Coming out is scary but worth it. Being able to be who you are meant to be, there's just nothing that compares.

Coming out as gay, lesbian, bisexual, or transgender is not about being "tolerated." You tolerate traffic or a bad toothache. It is about being true to yourself. You cannot be honest with others when you are not honest with yourself. Being miserable and hiding behind a mask takes a toll on you, and it definitely affects your relationships with the people you care about.

I personally know how immobilizing the fear of rejection can be, but among those who reject you will stand those who support you. The best thing you can do is surround yourself with a support system, because it may not be a smooth ride.

I won't lie—not everyone will respond the way you want them to. The people who you think will react one way may react another way. Those who love you, though, will stand by you, because they know who you are, and being gay, lesbian, bisexual, or transgender is just one part of your whole person.

Age: 26
Gender: Male
Race: Asian
Ethnicity: Filipino

If being gay wasn't natural, then it wouldn't exist. There's nothing wrong with you; it's not a disease or a defect. You can try to take a square peg and shove it into a round hole, but you won't be able to do it without losing a part of it. So why would you cut part of yourself off, just to fit into a society that may or may not do shit for you? My view on this whole coming-out thing is that you find out that a lot of people don't really matter. Yeah, they might be your friends now, but when the rubber meets the road, are they still going to be here? Most of my friends have proven that they would; those are the people you want to keep around, because at the end of the day, those are the people who are going to be there for you through all of this.

Try not to worry about how people will react. Just tell them, and then deal with it as it comes. Some people's reactions will be really unexpected, because there are some people who will embrace you with open arms, who you never thought would. That's not really a gay/straight thing. If someone doesn't accept you for who you are, that's just a shitty friend. Move on! It hurts, and it sucks, but just move on with your life like you're taking out the trash.

Also, look around at your friends, because chances are that you have another gay friend somewhere. See how your straight friends react to them, and it will be a good indicator of how well you'll be received by the rest of them too.

Age: 74
Gender: Female
Race: White
Ethnicity: American

I am a Protestant who was raised Southern Baptist in Texas but now am a member of Unity Church and a licensed Unity teacher.

When I was about age forty-five and married, with three children in their early twenties, I came to the conclusion (slowly) that my marriage was coming to an end. (My husband was in love/lust with another woman, and I was falling in love with a woman!)

I struggled internally for a couple of years over what to do. I did not want to break up the family, but I was getting more and more depressed. When I finally decided to leave my marriage and partner with a woman, I struggled with decisions such as should I tell my parents, my children, my friends? If so, what to say? This was difficult, even though I was a "mature adult."

I am so glad I decided to tell my children first, then parents, and lastly friends. After all those years of advising my children to tell the truth, I did not want to be dishonest! It took time for everyone to adjust to the divorce and Mother being gay, but eventually everyone came around to being a loving, accepting family again.

P. S.: A few years later, one of my daughters came out as a lesbian. She knew she could talk to me and my partner (her "bonus mom") easily.

Age: 29
Gender: Queer girl
Race: White
Ethnicity: German/English

I grew up in Austin, Texas. On the outside, I fit in. I knew how to follow the rules; I knew how to be a good student, band member, Lutheran, etc. I knew how to make my family proud of me.

When I realized why I felt different and finally found an identity that fit me, that I was queer, I was afraid that the only reason I'd been accepted was because of the rules I followed. I was afraid that living as myself would mean that everything I had built for myself would be gone. I was afraid that everything I'd wanted for myself—a family and kids and career—would never happen.

What I found was that people loved me because of who I am, and that I could have a full and happy life, including a family and kids. I was afraid to reach out to others for fear of rejection, but what I needed the most was community. As soon as I got connected with people who supported and loved the whole, full me, my life started to look like what I had always wanted for myself. Be brave! You are wonderful, and people will see that.

Age: 31
Gender: Female
Race: White/Latina
Ethnicity: Half Mexican, half Swiss-German

Do your best to try and find somebody that you can talk to. I know that can be hard, but just try to be observant of someone in your community. Maybe it's a teacher, maybe it's a counselor, or a neighbor; somebody that you can talk to so that you don't feel alone.

If you do have some kind of a strong spirituality or faith, then I would say pray about it, because the great thing is that God's on your side. God wants you to be happy. God is not out for you to be miserable, and He would not have made you with a heart that loves the same sex if He didn't want you that way. He would not make a mistake.

So you need to have some kind of community, a healthy community. It helps to move to a big city, and whatever you do, don't pretend that you're heterosexual and go get married! Don't be afraid to discover your heart. When I allowed myself to really explore what it meant to love somebody, the depth of it was never-ending, and it doesn't just have to be physical. It can be so wonderful just to experience the incredible beauty of the touch of someone's hand or be in their presence. So don't be afraid to love and really explore what that means and looks like for you.

Age: 24
Gender: Male
Race: White
Religion: Catholic

Coming out has helped me learn to love myself more, which is important for anyone, whether they're gay or straight. The other thing is that you start accepting other people for who they are and become nonjudgmental. We're all in this world together, and everyone's just doing the best that they can. You can't judge someone for being who they are, even if it's something you don't understand. You just learn to accept everyone and love everyone.

We all have a limited amount of time here on earth, and we're all sharing in our sorrows and joys and suffering together. So, is what you're doing making life better or making it worse? As hard as it's been for me to come out, and as much as I've suffered because of that, I don't want to see other people suffer; it makes me want to help other people through that.

The main advice I have is that you have control over when and who you tell. So, start with the people you know will support you and accept you, and then just slowly work your way up from there. If you're not ready for it, then you don't have to tell them. Just being able to verbally say, "I'm gay" or "I'm lesbian" is really important, because if you're not okay saying that, then you're still not okay with yourself. You just need to build up that confidence.

The last thing I want to say is that there's nothing wrong with you. Sexuality is fluid, and there's no right or wrong. It's not black and white. Part of loving yourself is being able to be in tune with your sexuality and be aware of what you're feeling and who you are. You just have to accept and embrace and love yourself.

Age: 24
Gender: Male
Race: Asian
Ethnicity: Filipino

I was born and raised in the Philippines. We moved to the United States when I was twelve. Practicing Christian.

"So, you've been getting into this gay life lately. How's that going?" my mom asked, while we were having lunch at a Johnny Rocket's one summer's day. The question caught me by surprise. I had been hinting for months prior to this encounter, hoping and praying that I would be relieved of the burden of coming out. Assured of her support and affirmed by her unconditional love, I breathed a sigh of relief. However, I knew that this was only the beginning.

Growing up in the Catholic Church, I knew my sexuality would be at odds with my spirituality. How does one reconcile these two seemingly dichotomous ideas? Existential questions like this plagued me. At first, my response was to compartmentalize the two identities, essentially living two separate lives; but doing so only exacerbated the shame I felt deep inside.

Faced with adversity, I can hear my mom's voice resound in my head, reminding me to let go and let God. So I did; I returned to my faith, to my God. Regardless of what people may say, my relationship with God remains steadfast and unchanged. I spent the following months in prayer and meditation. Through it all, I learned that sexuality—homosexuality included—is a gift from God, and that each of us is fearfully and wonderfully made.

What I didn't realize then—and what I know now—is that a spectrum of Christianity, or of religiosity for that matter, exists and abounds. What we see most often in the media—clips of Maggie Gallagher of National Organization for Marriage fame and televangelist Pat Robertson—are the most outspoken and extreme opinions regarding homosexuality. Don't let this discourage you. Instead, let it serve as an example that we need to strengthen our resolve. We need to continually sow seeds of love where there is hate, hope where there is despair, and light where there is darkness.

Conclusion

Every day, the world is changing for the better. With every passing moment, it becomes a safer, more accepting, and more loving place for gay people to let their lights shine brightly and proudly proclaim to the world who they are. The evidence is everywhere! Target, Subaru, and JC Penney unashamedly feature gay-positive ads for their companies. Kurt and Blaine had their epic first kiss on *Glee*. George Takei, Lady Gaga, Kathy Griffin, President Obama, Ellen DeGeneres, and so many others boldly proclaim our inherent right to love who we are and who we were born to be.

At this time in history, the gay community has just won two historic Supreme Court cases: one that allows the right for same-sex marriages to resume in California, and the other that requires the federal government to recognize all same-sex marriages in states where it is currently legal. As wonderful, encouraging, and inspiring as all of these changes are, though, you must remember that *you* are ultimately the one who holds the power to love yourself and whomever else you choose, whether the outside world affirms it or not.

You only have two choices in life: you can choose to live in fear, always worrying about what others will think of you and putting your needs aside to make other people comfortable, or you can choose to live in love, with the awareness that your needs and your life are just as important as everyone else's. You can either be happy and live your life, knowing that not everyone will be pleased (but they will probably get over it), or you can stay trapped in fear and watch your life pass you by. Someone once said, "If you care about what others think of you, you're saying that 'What you think of me is more important than what I think of myself.'" In the end, your opinion is the only one that matters. When you believe in your own self-worth, you can accomplish anything, but *you* are the only one with the power to make you love yourself.

Everyone has their own individual coming-out story, and some people may face more challenges than others on their journey. One day, though, you will realize that every person or institution that ever told you that you are not perfect just the way you are has become one of your greatest teachers. They are the ones that taught you that you cannot believe everything people tell you. They are the ones that will teach you to become independent of the opinions of others. The people who try to teach you "truths" that you know to be untrue are the ones you have to thank for the critical thinker you are or will become. They are the ones who taught you to overcome your fear of rejection and shamelessly express yourself, loving whomever you choose, redefining gender and gender roles, defying societal norms, and loving yourself completely and joyfully. The more adversity you face on your journey toward unconditional self-love, the more opportunities you have to grow and work out your courage muscles. By the time you realize the bliss of truly loving who you are, no one in the world will be able to bring you down.

You will learn to surround yourself with people who love and accept you without question, and you will lovingly remove yourself from the negative energy of people who do not. You will attract the perfect career into your life, where you can flourish, be yourself openly, and share your gifts and talents without fear of being fired for who you are. You will even find the perfect partner if you wish it, someone who makes your heart laugh and will help you continue to grow throughout your beautiful life.

Even though it is not always easy at first, coming out is an act of bravery, and there is nothing like freeing yourself from that dark and lonely closet. After you take that courageous first step of coming out to yourself, the universe will continue to support you and surround you with the people who will help you continue on the path toward inner peace and self-love. Unconditional love for yourself really is the only way to achieve inner peace. Love is who you truly are, and where real love exists, fear cannot. Just remember that it *is* okay to be afraid, even terrified! Bravery is being afraid to love and doing it anyway. You are perfect, beautiful, and whole right now, and the most important journey you will ever have in your life is finding your way back to remembering that.

Good luck on your coming-out journey, courageous, beautiful soul. Do not forget to surround yourself with the people who will lift you up when you're down and be there with you to celebrate every victory. When it comes to coming out, the good always outweighs the bad, no matter what. Being gay will cause you to grow into a far greater person than you ever thought possible, and that inner strength and love for yourself and others will carry you through the rest of your enlightened and love-filled future. You are on a journey from fear to fabulous, and it has only just begun.

Appendix A

Proposal to Start a GLBT and Straight Student Support Group at the Student Catholic Center

Mission statement:

This group's mission is to create a safe and accepting environment for gay, lesbian, bisexual, transgendered, and straight Catholic students to learn, discuss, share, and find support around issues related to homosexuality and spirituality.

Who: GLBT and straight Catholic students

This student group is for any of God's gay, lesbian, bisexual, transgendered (GLBT), and straight children at the University Catholic Center seeking to be loved and accepted as children of God.

What: A place for GLBT and straight Catholics to meet in a safe environment to discuss and receive peer support and love regarding issues related to homosexuality and spirituality in a Catholic setting

This group will be a place where young Catholic students can meet to talk about the love that God has for them and seek support from others who have had the experience of feeling isolated, marginalized, or a sense of not belonging in the Catholic Church. It will be a place for GLBT and straight Catholics to come home to after having had a bad experience with discrimination from a lay person, priest, sister, or deacon who may have misunderstood the Church's teaching that homosexuality is not something that someone chooses. This group will focus on the teachings of the Church document "Always Our Children" which speaks of "accepting the full truth of God's revelation about the dignity of the human person and the meaning of human sexuality; [and that] within the Catholic moral vision there is no contradiction among these levels of acceptance, for truth and love are not opposed."[1]

Where: At the Student Catholic Center in a Paulist environment

Having such a group as is being proposed could not have a better chance of success than on a college campus in a Paulist church. The Paulist Fathers' mission is to "enter into God's action of seeking out the lost, the alienated, the hurt, and the broken, [and] minister especially in welcoming people back to the Church."[2] The goal of the proposed group directly reflects this Paulist mission and provides a perfect segue for attracting students back to the Church who may have felt ostracized and invisible in church in the past. Additionally, the safe and nonjudgmental setting of the group will help to create a safe environment for students who would not otherwise feel comfortable attending the group because of the fear of other students discovering a part of them that they themselves are still ashamed of.

When: Bi-monthly and during the students' formative college years

This group will be available for students at a critical point in their development of identity and sense of self. College is not only a time when students decide what they want to do for the rest of their life, but it is also a time for them to develop a sense of who they will be for the rest of their life. Because being gay, lesbian, bisexual, or transgendered is such an important component of these students' self-identity, it is critical for them to find acceptance and love as a total being, sexuality and all. This is especially true within a church setting; because if there is only one place for a person to experience Christ's unconditional love it should be among followers of Jesus.

Why: To give GLBT Catholics a sense of belonging and support within the Church and to give insight to their straight peers about the challenges and struggles that GLBT Catholics face

The main reason for the formation of this group is to create a place that GLBT and straight Catholic students alike can call home within the University Catholic Center. So many gay and lesbian Catholic young people have expressed the unfortunate feeling that being gay and being Catholic cannot be in harmony with one another. They have been made to feel that they are a mistake that God has made, or that they are an inherent evil, by those who are ignorant of what the Church teaches about homosexuals as human beings and children of God. This group's purpose is to help GLBT students reconcile their spirituality with their sexuality, as well as give them a place to find support from other straight and GLBT Catholic students. This group will also serve to give some insight to straight Catholic students on the struggles that many GLBT Catholics face when they encounter discrimination and homophobia within their families, work, school, and faith communities.

How: Discuss Church documents, movies, and dialogue about Church teachings on homosexuality

One of the ways that the mission statement of this group will be carried out will be to first invite heterosexual and homosexual students to join the group and discuss various Church documents and teachings on the subject of homosexuality. There will be new topics of discussion for each meeting and students will also have the opportunity to bring up and discuss topics that they feel are important to furthering their spiritual development. This group's other main goal, which will permeate all of the meetings and discussions, is that of supporting the students with Christ-like love and acceptance while they cope with the challenge and opportunity that God has bestowed upon them as His GLBT and straight sons and daughters.

Appendix B

"The Heterosexual Questionnaire" by Martin Rochlin

The following questionnaire reverses some of the most common questions asked of gay people by those who do not understand homosexuality. These questions can prove useful in providing insight, understanding, and a sense of common ground between the gay and straight communities.

1. What do you think caused your heterosexuality?
2. When and how did you first decide you were a heterosexual?
3. Is it possible that your heterosexuality is just a phase you may grow out of?
4. Is it a possibility that your heterosexuality stems from a neurotic fear of others of the same sex?
5. If you've never slept with a person of the same sex, is it possible that all you need is a good gay lover?
6. To whom have you disclosed your heterosexual tendencies?
7. Why do you heterosexuals feel compelled to seduce others into your lifestyle?

8. Why do you insist on flaunting your heterosexuality? Can't you just be what you are and keep it quiet?

9. Would you want your children to be heterosexual, knowing the problems they'd face?

10. A disproportionate majority of child molesters are heterosexuals. Do you consider it safe to expose your children to heterosexual teachers?

11. Even with all the societal support marriage receives, the divorce rate is spiraling. Why are there so few stable relationships among heterosexuals?

12. Why do heterosexuals place so much emphasis on sex?

13. Considering the menace of overpopulation, how could the human race survive if everyone were heterosexual?

14. Could you trust a heterosexual therapist to be objective? Don't you fear that the therapist might be inclined to influence you in the direction of his or her own leanings?

15. How can you become a whole person if you limit yourself to compulsive, exclusive heterosexuality and fail to develop your natural, healthy homosexual potential?

16. There seem to be very few happy heterosexuals. Techniques have been developed that might enable you to change if you really want to. Have you considered trying aversion therapy?

Resources

LGBTQ Youth
- Gay, Lesbian and Straight Education Network—*www.glsen.org*
- Jump Start Your GSA!—*http://glsen.org/jumpstart*
- The Trevor Project—*www.thetrevorproject.org*
- "Think Before You Speak" Campaign—*www.thinkb4youspeak.com*
- Spiritual Pride Project—*www.spiritualprideproject.org*

Crisis Intervention and Suicide Prevention
- The Trevor Project—*www.thetrevorproject.org*
- The Born This Way Foundation—*www.bornthiswayfoundation.org/help*
- "It Gets Better" project—*www.itgetsbetter.org*

Religion and Spirituality
- *You Can Heal Your Life* by Louise L. Hay
- Soulforce—*www.soulforce.org*
- My Out Spirit— *www.myoutspirit.com*
- *For the Bible Tells Me So,* documentary—available for purchase on Amazon.com

- *What the Bible* Really *Says About Homosexuality* by Daniel Helminiak
- *HayHouseRadio.com*

Resources for Family and Friends
- PFLAG: Parents, Families and Friends of Lesbians and Gays—*www.PFLAG.org*[1]
- Atticus Circle—*www.atticuscircle.org*[2]
- *Princess Free Zone* blog and articles—
  "Don't Fear Your Child's Fearlessness"—
  http://princessfreezone.com/pfz-blog/2012/9/25/dont-fear-your-childs-fearlessness.html

  "You're Her Mother. You Can Say No."—
  http://princessfreezone.com/pfz-blog/2012/7/11/youre-her-motheryou-can-say-no.html

- *Bullied: What Every Parent, Teacher, and Kid Needs to Know about Ending the Cycle of Fear* by Carrie Goldman

LGBTQ Health
LGBTQ-friendly health providers—
  GLMA—
  www.glma.org/index.cfm?fuseaction=Page.viewPage&pageId=938&parentID=534&nodeID=1

Gay and bisexual men's health—
  Mayo Clinic—
  www.mayoclinic.com/health/health-issues-for-gay-men/MY00738

Centers for Disease Control—
www.cdc.gov/msmhealth/

Lesbian and bisexual women's health—
Centers for Disease Control—
www.cdc.gov/lgbthealth/women.htm

Women's Health.gov—
http://womenshealth.gov/publications/our-publications/fact-sheet/lesbian-bisexual-health.cfm

Transgender people's health—
GLMA—
www.glma.org/index.cfm?fuseaction=Page.viewPage &pageId=948&grandparentID=534&parentID= 938&nodeID=1

Centers for Disease Control—
www.cdc.gov/lgbthealth/transgender.htm

LGBT youth health—
Centers for Disease Control—
www.cdc.gov/lgbthealth/youth-resources.htm

Centers for Disease Control—
www.cdc.gov/healthyyouth/disparities/smy.htm

Centers for Disease Control—
www.cdc.gov/lgbthealth/youth.htm

Notes

Chapter 1

1. Alfred Kinsey. "Bisexuality." The Kinsey Institute for Research in Sex, Gender, and Reproduction, Inc. Accessed August 31, 2013, www.kinseyinstitute.org/resources/ak-data.html#bisexuality

Chapter 3

1. "The American Gay Rights Movement: A Timeline," Infoplease. com. © 2000–2013. Pearson Education, publishing as Infoplease. Accessed August 31, 2013, www.infoplease.com/ipa/A0761909.html.
2. Billy Hallowell. "5 Major Fears Gay Marriage Opponents Have about the Potential Nationwide Legalization of Same-Sex Unions." The Blaze.com. Accessed August 31, 2013, www.theblaze.com.
3. "State Nondiscrimination Laws in the US," TheTaskForce. org. National Gay and Lesbian Task Force. Accessed August 24, 2013, www.thetaskforce.org/downloads/reports/issue_maps/ non_discrimination_6_13_color.pdf.

Chapter 6

1. Sonia G. Austin, ed. "Erik Erikson." *Developmental Theories through the Life Cycle,* 2nd ed. New York: Columbia University Press, 2008, 45–50.
2. Joe Dispenza. *Breaking the Habit of Being Yourself: How to Lose Your Mind and Create a New One.* Carlsbad, California: Hay House, Inc., 2012.

3. Louise L. Hay. *You Can Heal Your Life.* Carlsbad, California: Hay House, Inc., 2004.

Chapter 8

1. Anonymous. *A Course in Miracles.* Tiburon, California: Foundation for Inner Peace, 1976.
2. Ibid.
3. Ibid.

Chapter 9

1. Refer to note 1 in chapter 3.
2. Elizabeth Kübler-Ross. *On Death and Dying: What the Dying Have to Teach Doctors, Nurses, Clergy, and Their Own Families.* New York: Scribner, 1969.
3. "LGBT-Sexual Orientation." American Psychiatric Association. © 2012. American Psychiatric Association, 2012. Web. Accessed August 24, 2013. <http://www.psychiatry.org/lgbt-sexual-orientation>
4. "1,500 animal species practice homosexuality: Homosexuality is quite common in the animal kingdom, especially among herding animals. Many animals solve conflicts by practicing same gender sex." News-Medical.Net. Accessed August 31, 2013, www.news-medical.net.
5. Refer to note 3 in chapter 9.
6. Refer to note 3 in chapter 9.
7. Home page. The Trevor Project. Accessed August 23, 2013, www.thetrevorproject.org.

Chapter 10

1. Gregory M. Herek. "Internalized Homophobia among Gay Men, Lesbians, and Bisexuals." *Readings for Diversity and Social Justice: An Anthology on Racism, Antisemitism, Sexism, Heterosexism, Ableism, and Classism.* Ed. Maurianne Adams, Warren J. Blumenfeld, Rosie

Castaneda, Heather W. Hackman, Madeline L. Peters, and Ximena Zuniga. New York: Routledge, 2000, 281–283.

2. "Internalized Homophobia." *Wikipedia: The Free Encyclopedia.* Accessed July 14, 2013, http://en.wikipedia.org/wiki/ Homophobia#Internalized_homophobia.

3. Refer to note 1 in chapter 8.

Chapter 11

1. Nicholas Ray. "Lesbian, Gay, Bisexual, and Transgender Youth: An Epidemic of Homelessness." National Gay and Lesbian Task Force Policy Institute and the National Coalition for the Homeless, 2006. Accessed August 23, 2013, www.thetaskforce.org/downloads/ reports/reports/HomelessYouth.pdf.

2. "LGBT Homeless." NationalHomeless.org. The National Coalition for the Homeless. Accessed August 23, 2013, www.nationalhomeless. org/factsheets/lgbtq.html.

3. Trevor Lifeline page. TheTrevorProject.org. Accessed August 23, 2013, www.thetrevorproject.org/pages/get-help-now.

4. Get Help Now page. BornThisWayFoundation.org. Accessed August 23, 2013, www.bornthiswayfoundation.org/help.

Chapter 13

1. Home page. MyOutSpirit.com: Come Out Spiritually. Goko Media, LLC, nd. Accessed August 31, 2013, myoutspirit.com.

Chapter 14

1. United States Conference of Catholic Bishops Committee on Marriage and Family. "Always Our Children: A Pastoral Message to Parents of Homosexual Children and Suggestions for Pastoral Ministers." Washington, D.C.: United States Catholic Conference, Inc., 1997.

2. Daniel A. Helminiak. *What the Bible Really Says about Homosexuality.* San Francisco: Alamo Square Press, 1994. Also, *For the Bible Tells Me So,* dir. Daniel Karslake. First Run Features, 2007. Refer to note

1 in chapter 13. Resources page. "Soulforce: Relentless Nonviolent Resistance." Soulforce.org. N.P. Accessed August 25, 2013, www.soulforce.com/resources.

Chapter 15

1. Christopher Bagley and Pierre Tremblay. "Elevated Rates of Suicidal Behavior in Gay, Lesbian, and Bisexual Youth." *Crisis: The Journal of Crisis Intervention and Suicide Prevention*, 21.3, (2000): 111-117. Accessed September 2, 2013. doi: 10.1027//0227-5910.21.3.111.
2. J. G. Kosciw, E. A. Greytak, M. J. Bartkiewicz, M. J. Boesen, and N. A. Palmer. "The 2011 National School Climate Survey: The Experiences of Lesbian, Gay, Bisexual, and Transgender Youth in Our Nation's Schools." New York: GLSEN, 2012. Accessed August 23, 2013, www.glsen.org.
3. Refer to note 3 in chapter 11.

Chapter 16

1. Lydia Saad. "In U.S., 52% Back Law to Legalize Gay Marriage in 50 States." Gallup Politics. Accessed August 21, 2013, www.gallup.com/poll/163730/back-law-legalize-gay-marriage-states.aspx.
2. Refer to note 1 in chapter 3.
3. Martin Rochlin. "The Heterosexual Questionnaire." N.P., 1972.
4. Home page. ThinkB4YouSpeak.com. GLSEN and the Ad Council, 2008. Accessed August 15, 2013, ThinkB4YouSpeak.com.
5. "Legalize Gay." AmericanApparel.net. Accessed September 1, 2013, www.americanapparel.net/legalizegay.
6. "About Gay? Fine by Me." AtticusCircle.org. Accessed September 1, 2013, www.atticuscircle.org/about-gay-fine-by-me.
7. About page. NOH8 Campaign. Accessed September 1, 2013, www.noh8campaign.com/article/about.
8. The Campaign Page. "About the Campaign." SafeSpace.GLSEN.org. Accessed August 15, 2013, SafeSpace.GLSEN.org.
9. Jump Start Your GSA Page. "Welcome to the GLSEN Jump-Start Guide!" GLSEN.org. Accessed August 15, 2013, http://glsen.org/jumpstart.

10. 1Refer to note 3 in chapter 14.

Chapter 17

1. Home Page. Amazon.com. Accessed September 2, 2013, www.amazon.com.
2. Marcy Michaels and Marie Desalle. *The Lowdown on Going Down: How to Give Her Mind-Blowing Oral Sex.* New York: Broadway Books, 2005.
3. Douglas Adams. *The Hitchhiker's Guide to the Galaxy.* New York: Pocket Books, 1979.
4. Home Page. Planned Parenthood. Accessed August 31, 2013, www.plannedparenthood.org.
5. "Lesbian, Gay, Bisexual and Transgender Health." Centers for Disease Control and Prevention. CDC 24/7: Saving Lives. Protecting People. Accessed August 15, 2013, www.cdc.gov/lgbthealth/index.htm.
6. Resources for Patients Page. "Find a Provider." GLMA: Health Professionals Advancing LGBT Equality. Accessed August 15, 2013, www.glma.org/index.cfm?fuseaction=Page.viewPage&pageId=534.

Appendix A

1. See note 1 in chapter 14.
2. "Mission Statement." The Paulist Fathers: Giving the Word a Voice. Accessed September 2, 2013, www.paulist.org/about/mission-statement.

Resources

1. Home Page. PFLAG: Parents, Families and Friends of Lesbians and Gays. Accessed September 2, 2013, www.PFLAG.org.
2. Home Page. Atticus Circle: Stand Up Straight for Equal Rights. Accessed September 2, 2013, www.atticuscircle.org.

Acknowledgments

Throughout the years, so many people have provided the inspiration, love, and wisdom that have made this project possible. I am eternally grateful to my parents, Mary Jane and Stanley, for their never-ending supply of unconditional love, encouragement, wise advice, and positive energy, and to my sisters, Christina and Heather, for being the best sisters anyone could ask for and always loving me for who I am. I wouldn't be where I am today without you.

Many thanks to my friend Andrew, for giving me the initial prompting I needed to turn my idea of writing a coming-out guide into a reality, and to all of my wonderful family and friends who have been so willing to give me advice and feedback throughout my writing process: Auntie Alicia, Natalie, S.J., Keith, Gina, Jodi, Eugene, KJ, Idzel, John, Femi, Andrea, Saul, Kristin, and Leesa.

A special thanks to my dear friends Jacky, Kristy, and Nichole for their endless supply of hugs, love, listening ears, and humor that helped me through some of the darkest and scariest times in my coming-out process; Amber Baldwin, the wonderful therapist who enabled me to break through the ingrained internalized homophobia that was holding me back and finally reach a state of unconditional self-love; my uncle Mike, my sister Heather, and S.J. for all of their expert advice and assistance with my book cover design; and my soul sister, Kristy Lines, for donating her professional skills and taking my beautiful author photo.

The outpouring of love and laughter that I receive from my incredible grandparents, Ann and Paul Bullinger, aunts, uncles, and cousins is completely inspiring, and I am so blessed to have you all in my life.

Much of what I have accomplished over the past decade would not have happened without the fearless and generous support of the 2007–2008 staff at the University Catholic Center, especially from Dave Farnum, Fr. Ed Koharchik, Fr. Ed Novak, and Michelle Goodwin. Thank you for the unconditional love you have shown to every student who has walked through the doors of the Catholic Center and for your outpouring of support and willingness to help Prism move past any challenges or roadblocks it has encountered in the past.

I would additionally like to acknowledge everyone who has been a great teacher and inspiration on my spiritual journey, as well as on my coming-out journey: Sarah Kyle, Suze Miller, Louise Hay, Karen McCrocklin, Cheryl Richardson, Ellen DeGeneres, Portia de Rossi, Wayne Dyer, and, of course, my mom.

Finally, I need to express my infinite gratitude to all of the friends, coworkers, and youth who have honored me by sharing their coming-out stories with me or coming to me for advice in the past. You are the reason I have written this book, and it is my hope that many more people will benefit from the lessons of courage and wisdom that you all have taught me and allowed me to experience with you.

I love you all to my core.

About the Author

Chelsea Griffo is an author, licensed master social worker, Applied Behavioral Analysis therapist, and activist for LGBTQ self-love and empowerment. Over the years, she has been deeply involved in the LGBTQ community as a volunteer support group facilitator for LGBTQ youth, a community activist, conference and event organizer, and a creator and advocate of safe spaces for LGBTQ people to express and develop their spirituality.

Empowering people to love themselves, embrace who they were born to be, and realize their personal greatness is Chelsea's life passion. She received her undergraduate and graduate education from the School of Social Work at the University of Texas at Austin.